654

D1500009

THE TROUBLED CONTINENT

Books by DOUGLAS HYDE

The Answer to Communism

I Believed

Red Star versus the Cross (with Father Dufay)

The Mind behind New China

One Front across the World

God's Bandit

The Peaceful Assault

United We Fall

Confrontation in the East

Dedication and Leadership

One-room homes of Lima's "shantytown" line steep hillside.

by Douglas Hyde

THE
TROUBLED
CONTINENT

A New Look at Latin America

PFLAUM PRESS DAYTON, OHIO 1967

F
1414.2
.H9
1967

Contents

List of Illustrations

Frontispiece: One-room homes of Lima's "shantytown" line steep hillside.

Prologue

The first time I went to Latin America I looked around and said to myself, "If I were still a Communist and had been sent here to organize the Communist Party, what a wonderful assignment this would be." Almost everything that the Communist in such circumstances would look for was there already, just waiting to be exploited. All the ingredients of political dynamite were lying ready to hand. Bring them together and the flash would follow almost automatically.

Extremes of wealth and poverty existing shamelessly and provocatively side by side.

Mass unemployment, low wages, and incredibly bad housing conditions in the towns.

Hundreds of thousands of slum dwellers, natural gun fodder for any revolution, encircling every great city.

Turbulent, politically-minded students living in huge hostels situated right at each city's heart.

Land-hungry peasants working on, or living adjacent to, vast and often uncultivated estates owned by absentee landlords.

A small, ultra-conservative ruling class almost devoid of social conscience, clinging arrogantly, and against all the lessons of our day, to a way of life which had its roots in human deprivation and suffering.

Widespread nationalism increasingly taking the form of anti-imperialism and, more specifically, of suspicion and detestation of the United States, the big, heavy-handed neighbor to the north.

An established tradition of violence as a means of solving political problems and of removing political opponents.

A culture based on a religion identified with the rich and powerful, ill understood by the vast majority of common folk and practiced by only a minority.

What more could a Communist want?

*   *   *

While I was making preparations to go to a conference in Panama in 1955, I learned that the President of the Republic had been assassinated at the racetrack. I wondered momentarily whether I should unpack again. Would the situation there be too unsettled for the conference to be held at all? I need not have worried.

When I got to Panama, I found that the incident had affected the life of practically no one outside the 200 ruling families who spend their time juggling for power and position.

The Catholic Rural Life Movement of the United States, with the encouragement of the Holy See, had convened the conference in order to assist the growth and organization of credit unions and producers' co-operatives and to prepare the way for agrarian reform. To it came socially-minded bishops, priests, and laymen, trade union and peasant leaders, people active in movements for reform throughout the Caribbean, from all over Central America, and from much of South America.

From this conference came the beginnings of a Central American and Caribbean federation of co-operative societies and credit unions. When it was over, I flew up to a small jungle town for a demonstration of *campesinos*. From miles around came large numbers of peasants, mainly Indians, who were members of producers' co-operative societies. They traveled in from all the surrounding villages, then marched together carrying with them the products of their co-operative efforts.

The march ended with the celebration of Mass on the steps of a ruined Spanish colonial church in which no Mass had been said for generations. At one point the demonstrators were asked to hold up the products of their labors in order that they might be blessed. Up went hundreds of small, squawking, bantam-sized chickens, bowls of corn, rice, and beans. As the bishop standing at the altar concluded his benediction, a little, dark-faced Indian woman standing at my side lifted an undersized chicken up to her face, almost touching her lips with its beak, and murmured: "Little chicken, life will never again be the same for either of us."

The work we had been doing had the approval of the new President of the Republic. He had sent one of his ministers to attend the demonstration. Yet, when I opened my paper in Panama City next morning, I read that, even while our demonstration was taking place, not far away a trade union organizer had been arrested for trying to form a labor union among plantation workers.

A group of us went along to the presidential palace to

protest that this sort of thing made nonsense of what we were trying to do. It conflicted strangely, we said, with the President's assurances of support for our aims.

Patiently the President explained to us that it was not his police who had arrested the organizer nor was it his territory, even though this was within the Republic of Panama. The arrested man had been trying to organize a labor union on United Fruit Company territory, he told us, "and my writ does not run there. It was not my police who arrested him, but I will negotiate to see if I can obtain his release."

*   *   *

The riots had already begun when I arrived in Santiago de Chile in 1957. It was the old story: runaway inflation which the Government had said it would end by pegging wages, prices, and profits. They had pegged the wages, but prices and profits had been allowed to continue to soar. Then, putting match to tinder and going against everything that it had promised, the Government itself had raised the fares on its state-owned buses.

Crowds of students had begun to stone the buses in the streets, then turned one or two over and set fire to them. Police had then opened fire and succeeded in killing a girl student who was in no way connected with the agitation. A pious little girl, she was coming away from a meeting of the Legion of Mary when she was shot down. There was clearly a lot more trouble to come. It came.

The lumpen-proletariat, rootless and propertyless, with nothing to lose and nothing to defend, came pouring from the slums into the city, rioting, looting, destroying. Day after day the police opened fire. They killed so many people that in the end the mere sight of a policeman became a provocation in itself.

A state of siege was declared, and, too late, the President called the police off the streets. The only trouble was that though this ended their provocation, the military who should have replaced them failed to show up for several hours. (Later, there were courts-martial because of this, and at these it was said that the crack regiment concerned had mutinied.) In the meantime the mob took possession of the heart of the city. Spokesmen of the illegal Communist party suddenly emerged from the underground and, displaying impressive qualities of leadership, quickly turned the seemingly uncontrollable mob into an organized force.

For days there were tanks and armored cars at every crossroads. Rifle and machine gun fire could be heard from morning till night. The military seemed almost as trigger-happy as the police had been, as I discovered when, breaking the curfew one night, I had to dodge behind a pillar to miss the hail of gunfire they aimed at me.

The official figure for those killed was, as I recall it, around 40. No one in Santiago accepted this, and with good reason. In almost every working-class suburb the funerals went on practically non-stop for ten days on end. I talked to one priest who in his parish alone had buried almost as many victims of the shooting as the Government claimed for the whole great city. At the end of it all, the Government had yielded nothing, conceded nothing. There was new repression, but no new reforms.

One morning near the end of the period of the riots I was breakfasting with Wolf Ladejinsky, the man who had been responsible for Japan's land reform and who had just flown in from Vietnam to attend the same Rural Life Con-

ference as I. A solitary, belated shot rang out from somewhere nearby. We had thought the shooting was already at
an end.

"The trouble about this damn place," said Wolf, "is
that nothing gives. It is true of all Latin America. That is
why, if they don't soon learn, some day it is going to snap,
and God help them then."

*   *   *

A few days later, still in Chile and almost before the
blood had been hosed off the streets of Santiago, I sat eating with a family on their great hacienda, only a few miles
outside the capital.

My host was urbane; his family, delightful; the atmosphere, relaxed. The conversation began with stories about
what life had been like at the Sorbonne in his day. Then it
switched to his children's experiences there and at other
European universities. Later we got round to the French
priest-worker experiment, the *Mission de Paris*, and from
there to current trends in French Catholic thought.

No one mentioned the riots, killings, and funerals in
nearby Santiago until I tried to steer the conversation in
that direction.

"Let's talk of more pleasant things," said my host with
a charming smile. "I know your own Catholic hierarchy
doesn't approve of the French Catholic *avant garde*, but am
I right in thinking that some of the Anglican clergy and lay
intellectuals follow closely what is happening there?"

*   *   *

Caracas, Venezuela, and all Latin America, too, seemed
in 1961 to be full of priests who had recently been expelled,

or had fled, from Cuba. Just about every one of them was now engaged in telling other Latin Americans about the catastrophe which so unexpectedly and undeservedly had hit Cuba and the Church. Cuba had, unlike some others, been a "good" Catholic country, they said. In Cuba, everyone had known the Church's social teachings because these had been practiced by rich and poor alike. Consequently, in Catholic Cuba there had been social justice until Fidel Castro and his rag-tag mob had come along and destroyed it. Yes, everyone had been prosperous and happy until Communism sneaked in by the back door in the guise of Castro's so-called social revolution.

For every priest who made such claims there were half a dozen laymen, exiled businessmen, professional people, erstwhile employers and landowners, to support him with stories of their own personal experiences and, in particular, their own personal losses.

I met one day a Cuban priest whom I had known in the past and whose sense of balance, in particular, I had deeply respected. Gone now were his superb objectivity, his quiet, factual approach to political questions, his charity toward the Church's opponents. Dazed, saddened, and carried along by the mounting stream of near-hysteria, he was repeating the same stories as the rest. Catholic Cuba had gone Communist because of Fidel Castro's perfidy. All Latin America would soon go the same way unless sufficient people immediately got into the fight against Godless Communism, or the United States went right in and smashed the Cuban Communist regime.

In that somewhat overheated, over-wrought atmosphere it was almost impossible to discover what was truth and what was fear-engendered fiction.

* * *

As I was about to fly from Venezuela down to British Guiana that same year, I bumped into an American who had just returned from the British colony. He was the leader of an organization which combined evangelism with the wilder forms of anti-Communism. British Guiana, he said, would very soon be another Cuba if the British Government was foolish enough to give it independence.

Already, Prime Minister Cheddi Jagan, backed by his vast Communist party, had some of Castro's men in British Guiana training thousands of Guianese in guerilla warfare.

As soon as independence came, they would, the American asserted in tones which left no room for debate, fan out all over Latin America, taking Red revolution with them. He totally ignored the fact that any such Guianese guerillas would be able to speak only English, although they would have to function in a Spanish- and Portuguese-speaking world.

He was now, he explained, on his way back to the U.S. to raise some more cash from the big industrialists who supported his crusade. Before seeing them, he was going to stop over at Washington, D.C., "to drum up some of the people in the State Department" and alert them to the danger.

* * *

The priest to whom I talked in Yucatan, Mexico, in 1960, was working in Graham Greene country. I had come to the land of The Lawless Roads and The Power and the Glory from British Honduras. This was the area where not long ago the Church was being persecuted.

The priest's soutane was green with age and threadbare. He was probably as poor as his people. Things were better now, he told me, but a clergyman would still be wise not to draw attention to himself.

Was he, I asked, trying to build up the Church again by finding new ways of making the Faith meaningful to the people such as, for example, by concerning himself with their social and economic problems?

He looked at me almost uncomprehendingly. No, he said, dully and dispiritedly, he was an ordinary priest working in a poor parish, just doing his job in a place where the only ones who ever came near the church were old women and adolescent girls.

"God knows," he said wearily, "that's difficult enough."

*   *   *

It was with memories such as these that I went back once more to Central and South America, looking for signs of political, social, and ecclesiastical change.

THE TROUBLED CONTINENT

The Flight South

1

My annual lecture tour of North American universities was over, and I was visiting old friends in New Orleans on my way south to Guatemala. From there I would travel on to other Latin American countries, renewing old friendships, making new contacts, revisiting places I had not seen for some years.

I was going there in search of signs of change. Not many years ago that would indeed have been an eccentric errand. Latin Americans themselves would have thought that I was on a wild goose chase. Over and over again, when I was making my first visit to Central America in 1955, they had told me: "You are in Latin America now. Things move very slowly here when they move at all."

Over the past ten years I had seen the first hint of the beginnings of change revealed at conferences I had attended, observed it at work in the minds of people I knew. But no one could say that this added up to enough to be really significant. What the immense material and spiritual needs of the people demanded urgently and imperatively

3

was that Latin America should be brought into the twentieth-century world.

Now, dozens of organizations, most of them North American, had been set up to assist precisely that process. I had helped some come into existence, had watched others. There were some which were trying to bring it about by persuasion and education. Some were using the political threat of Communism as a lever; others used the demographic and economic threats of present hunger and future over-population.

One Pittsburgh steel baron had told me a year or two earlier: "Latin America has to be brought into the twentieth century even though we have to drag her in kicking and screaming."

Such activities and approaches might be assisting to bring about change or, perhaps just as likely, they might be having the effect of hardening attitudes against it, confirming in their traditionalism and conservatism people who have a fierce pride in their own culture and in their independence and who fear that both are threatened by others who would hustle them into accepting an alien way of life.

For the outside observer like me, with the interests of a well-loved area at heart, there could at least be no doubt about the need for change, political, social, and ecclesiastical.

Ecclesiastical change, of course, is of exceptional importance in the Latin American context because, even though the Catholic Church throughout the sub-continent has for years been under attack from sections of its own people, and neglected by vastly more, its tremendous power to act as either a spur or a brake is undeniable.

THE NEW DISCOVERY

Most people today know that there has been at the United States Government level a considerable growth of interest in Latin American internal affairs and that this has found tangible expression in the Alliance for Progress, and in official and semi-official U.S. projects for speeding up the development of Latin American countries.

Few people outside North America have any idea of the mass of non-government organizations that have sprung up in the United States and the immense variety of voluntary activities which they have initiated, all on behalf of Latin America. For a surprising length of time Americans had been behaving as though they just did not know, or had no desire to know, the poverty-stricken foreigners who lived next door. They hardly acknowledged their existence, and so they accepted no responsibility for them.

One might at least have supposed that the huge U.S. Catholic community would have felt some sense of kinship with the 200,000,000 Latin Americans whom their Church claimed as Catholics. In practice U.S. Catholics had no more feeling for them than did the rest of the population.

Then came Castro, and what membership in the Mystical Body of Christ had notably failed to do, fear of Communism achieved almost overnight. One does not have to be cynical to see the origins of the new interest in Latin America in these terms. But it is necessary to add that, whatever its origins, it was not long before a movement had got under way which drew magnificently on the great and largely untapped reservoir of idealism that exists in the U.S. Once the needs of Latin America had been sharply brought home in terms which North Americans could understand, there was a rush of young idealists to go off to lend a hand in what might have been called "Operation Uplift."

Those who went were shocked to learn that almost next door to them lived millions of people who were illiterate, hungry, poverty-stricken, and disease-ridden. (Since then President Johnson has made them aware that, even within their own country, there are other millions who fall into the same categories, though their plight may not be so extreme.)

All the generosity and warm-heartedness of those who grasped the point, particularly the youngsters, was challenged. In that first period of the great awakening, the president of a Catholic girls' college in Massachusetts told me that 80 of that year's graduates had gone to Latin America as unpaid teachers or as social workers from her college alone. Just how qualified or prepared the volunteers were at that time is anybody's guess. But their going was immensely significant as a demonstration and an example.

From among the Catholic community, increasing numbers of small groups of priests and laymen began to head south. Cardinal Cushing of Boston, impulsive and generous, talked of hundreds, even thousands of priests being spared from his and other U.S. dioceses to work in Latin America. Almost every missionary society and religious order began to scrutinize the disposition of its members to see who could be spared for the work. They, like similar bodies all over the West, were under pressure from Rome to come to the aid of the Church in Latin America.

Rome's call was being heard in many lands. Spain began to send in more priests and promised that their numbers would quickly grow during the course of the next ten years. Priests came from Ireland, Holland, Germany, Belgium,

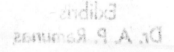

Italy, France, Britain, Malta, even the Philippines. In most cases bishops and religious superiors spared only a handful, but even so this was a gesture, an act of solidarity with the Latin American bishops, an expression of their belief that the soul of Latin America's 200,000,000 Catholics was at stake.

But the biggest response, as was to be expected, came from the United States. One could almost judge whether a diocese or a religious community was inward-looking or outward-turning by the degree of its awareness of Latin American needs.

Reverend mothers running schools in Kansas, remembering those few acres of land in Brazil which someone had bequeathed to them years ago, hurriedly began to draw up plans for schools, hospitals, social centers. Sisters who had never been outside their own state fell over each other to volunteer to work in countries far from home, and far from their experience too.

Lay missionaries, given the name of Papal Volunteers— and often using this even when they had no formal connection with the official Church movement of that name— turned up in one Latin American country after another. They had unbounded enthusiasm, but in those first days quite frequently they had few other qualifications; or, equally frequently, they were lacking those that were most needed.

The development of activity on behalf of Latin America within the Catholic Church in the United States was rather like that initiated at government level: it began with a generous, strongly felt, but poorly thought-out desire to do something, which tended to find expression in largely unplanned, uncoordinated, and ill-prepared action. Then, in due course, came attempts to achieve better organization and a deeper understanding of the actual needs of the area.

I was still discussing the needs of Latin America and the U.S. contribution to their solution when I had to say some hurried good-byes at the New Orleans airport, before boarding the Pan American jet which would take me to Guatemala City via Merida in Mexico.

THE LATIN AMERICAN APPROACH

Traveling on the same flight as I, was a student from Costa Rica. As it happened, he had just completed his studies at the Inter-American Center, New Orleans, where I had spent the last few days. When we got into conversation, I learned that the large black pipe he smoked was something of a symbol of his independence, a proof that he had not been Americanized. He explained that he saw pipe-smoking as an English rather than an American habit. As he surrounded himself with foul-smelling smoke, he told himself and the world that he, at least, although he had spent some time in the United States, had remained uncorrupted and unbrainwashed.

His views on Communism were ones I had heard expressed dozens of times before by young leaders in Africa and Asia. On this subject politically conscious Asia, Africa, and Latin America speak with almost one voice. He was, he said, neither anti- nor pro-Communist. He did not want his country to be dependent upon either the U.S.A. or the U.S.S.R. It should learn from both and trade with both. He was particularly glad that Costa Rica was now selling coffee to East Germany. Nothing was worse than for a country's main export to go to only one country, particularly if that country was the powerful United States which had for so long dominated the economies of the Central American republics.

Almost inevitably he called himself a socialist. This, one could take for granted. His sort of socialism, he said, was that of the British Labor party. He wanted evolutionary change, but he wanted it to come as quickly as possible.

The majority of students at his own university in Costa Rica—like his people generally—resented being told by the United States that they must be anti-Communist. Coming from such a source, this simply had the effect of making them more ready to listen to the Communists. Similarly, although many of his people thought the Alliance for Progress good, they still suspected it because of its emphasis on anti-Communism and because America had been prepared over the years to back any tyrant, dictator, corrupt politician, or businessman so long as he was anti-Communist.

The United States, he went on, had shown itself concerned only to support anti-Communists, without discriminating between good rulers and bad, and with no regard for whether they were for or against necessary social reforms. Current U.S. activities in Vietnam confirmed this completely for him. If you wanted proof that the U.S. leopard does not change its spots, there was all you needed in Vietnam at this moment.

Here, as I knew from the past and as I was to learn once more as I traveled from country to country throughout Latin America, was the authentic voice of a large section of educated, articulate young Latin Americans—the future leaders whom the United States is so eager to influence.

I suppose that many a North American tourist who has never in his life encountered a Communist would have

classified my traveling companion as a "Commie" or a
"Com-symp." The fact is that the views he expressed are
typical of those held by a large section of his generation.
That this does not make them Communist is reflected in
the fact that membership of the Communist party in his
own country of Costa Rica, for example, dropped from
3,000 members in 1947, when Communist popularity was
at its height, to a mere 300 six years later.

Typical, too, was his reaction to my questions about his
attitude toward religion. For him as a Latin American,
Christianity meant Catholicism. But this in turn meant the
Catholic Church toward which he showed the same de-
tached sort of tolerance that a once colonial, now independent country may feel toward the old colonial power.
He felt a closer link with the Church than with any other
religious institution and was prepared to admit some sort
of residual loyalty to it. "But," he emphasized, "I do not
like it when Americans talk of Jesus Christ as though He
were the founder of the American way of life, the free-enter-
prise society."

MEXICO'S WAY

When we stopped at Merida, in Yucatan, Mexico, my
companion from Costa Rica gave me his views of the progress that Mexico had made in recent years. What he liked
about Mexico, he said, was that it provided evidence that
Latin American countries could develop along democratic
lines which were also truly their own.

He was astonished when I told him that for many years
some people—particularly Catholics—in the U.S. and Europe regarded Mexico as a Communist country, as aston-

ished, in fact, as I had been when, after leaving the Communist party and coming to the Catholic Church, I heard my new co-religionists talking in these terms.

That some of the country's state governors had called themselves Marxists was, of course, undeniable. So, too, was the assertion that some of these had persecuted Catholics and that the country had gone through a violently anticlerical phase. But any Latin American can distinguish between anti-clericalism, no matter how bitter, and hostility to religion as such. And the more politically conscious of the younger generation can by now also distinguish between a revised and adapted Marxism and the Marxism of the Communists.

The Communist party of Mexico has, in fact, never been an outstandingly successful one. With probably not many more than 5,000 members, it is today regarded by Communists everywhere as one of the problem children in the Communist family. For nearly a quarter of a century its leaders have been deeply divided; this means that their differences arose long before the present split in the international movment.

Like the Communist party of Uruguay, the Mexican party has legal standing—and this is unusual in Latin America. And like it, too, it has little influence on its country's politics. Such influence as it has is among a few intellectuals and is exerted through Communist front organizations rather than in its own right.

Mexico's national and agrarian revolution may be said to have started when in 1810 the rural Mexican priest Father Miguel Hidalgo y Costilla led his peasants' protest march to Mexico City, voicing the downtrodden peasants' cry for help. He was executed, but his example helped to inspire the revolution which began in 1905 and lasted into recent years. That the revolution from time to time took ugly turns was, against the background of Mexico's history, perhaps inevitable. That a transformation of the entire social structure was required is undeniable.

Mexico's story in the first part of this century was one of continuing rebellion and revolution. In this it bears a certain superficial similarity to that of Ireland. And as in Ireland, too, the Communists today have relatively little success. Explaining their lack of progress in Ireland, Dublin's Communist leaders say that after years of revolution their people have for the time being exhausted their revolutionary potentialities. Communists may possibly say the same of Mexico.

But there are other powerful factors which work against the spread of Communism. Particularly important is the country's agrarian reform which is being made a reality for the large numbers of people who benefit by it. Between 1915 and 1963, 123,500,000 acres were distributed. More than 2,000,000 of this total were distributed in 1963, an indication that the agrarian revolution still continues.

No one need be surprised that anti-clericalism and indifference toward religion are to be found in Mexico, particularly in the urban areas and among the intellectuals. The wonder is that the Church has any following there at all. Spain's rows with Rome and her later maneuvering led to Mexico's Catholic community being cut off from the Holy See for years on end. By 1829 religion was in a perilous state, and there was not a single bishop left in the whole of Mexico.

For years after that the Church was involved in a head-on clash with the forces of progress and, therefore, identified with the forces of reaction. Officially organized opposition to the Church, which often had the appearance of hostility to all religion, continued for more than a century. From these years of trouble—and, indeed, assisted by them—the Church emerged materially weaker, but spiritually more vigorous than before. Now, for 20 years Church and State have lived together in an atmosphere of relative calm and tolerance despite the fact that the hostile legislation of the earlier period remains on the statute books.

Most of Mexico's 37,000,000 people regard themselves as Catholics today. Just how Catholic is another matter. A minority of them, organized in such bodies as the Christian Family Movement, are very good and extremely dynamic. If we are looking for the forces that make for change in Mexico, we may say that democracy there is more healthy than in many parts of Latin America; Catholicism, although battered by years of anti-clericalism, is a growing, increasingly relevant force; Communism, for the moment at least, comes near to being a stagnant one. These three facts are not unconnected.

Reaction and Revolution

2

An American priest to whom I had written when I decided to make Guatemala the starting point of my latest Latin American tour reminded me that I would be arriving on the Tuesday of Holy Week. "From then until Easter Monday," he wrote, "all governmental offices and business establishments are closed. People dedicate themselves particularly to the processions of Holy Week, which in Guatemala are some of the most famous in Latin America. You might say that you will see Catholicity at its best and at its worst."

As I made my way through Guatemala City's commercial center on the evening of my arrival, I found myself being jostled by men in purple hooded gowns hurrying off to take their place in the processions. Already, thousands of people were lining the route. There were noticeably few upper class, Spanish types among them. Almost all were either Mestizos or pure Indians. Some 53 per cent of the country's population of 4,100,000 are of Mayan and other Indian stock; 38 per cent are Mestizos. The proportion of Mestizos is highest in the cities, while the Indians form a majority in most rural areas.

Many of the women who had come either to participate in or to watch the processions were dressed in long, brightly-colored, hand-woven skirts and gay shawls. Small girls wearing long ankle-length skirts were at all the street corners doing a brisk trade in sweets and fruit.

On the following night I watched some of the processions as they made their way through the city streets. In what was described to me as one of the smaller processions, teams of 60 men took turns carrying a float on which was a great figure of Christ carrying His cross. It was illuminated by powerful lights connected to immensely heavy batteries.

After this came three statues of Our Lady of Sorrows, similarly mounted and illuminated. These were carried by teams of 40 women. New teams took over at each intersection. Thus hundreds of men and women were involved in carrying the floats in every one of the numerous processions.

Most of those who participated clearly saw this as an act of genuine devotion. This would be particularly true of the women. Somehow, as they staggered along under the weight of the great floats, they were identifying themselves with the suffering Christ as He staggered under the weight of His cross. They were relieving Him of some of His burden, sharing in His passion.

For a fairly large minority, I would judge, some degree of exhibitionism and even of social snobbery was mixed with religious sentiment. To be among the active participants carried with it a certain prestige, an assertion of importance in the local community.

It took me a day or two to realize that one effect of its being Holy Week was a significant two-way movement of population in and out of the city. While the Mestizos from the encircling slums and the Indians from the poverty-stricken rural areas were coming in for the processions, the wealthy "Spanish" types were streaming out in their big cars for holidays in the mountains or on the coast.

Each night the processions got longer, the crowds more numerous. By Good Friday the city was packed. An early morning stroll revealed that the proportion of Indians was by now immensely higher than before. It had become a city of the little people, of the urban and rural poor. The Indians and Mestizos took over Guatemala City, even as the rich took themselves off to the cool of the mountains or to their yachting and surf-riding.

With hardly a car to be seen, the little dark people jammed every street from wall to wall. They sat in shop doorways, in public squares and gardens, congregated in huge numbers around every church, eating, talking, quietly laughing together. Thousands went from church to church saying prayers in each. In particular, they gathered around the cathedral where they could watch the processions setting out or returning after hours of circulating in the streets.

In the afternoon, while the processions were fanning out all over the city, I went into the cathedral. It was dark and almost deserted. Even the statues had gone, leaving it curiously empty.

Many of the Spanish-style statues one sees in Latin American churches leave me ill at ease. Their creators have clearly dwelt with such immense concentration, and for so long, upon every minute detail of the physical aspects of the Passion that one is left asking at what point piety ends and sadism begins. Their tasteless, gaudy depiction of Christ's suffering seems at times to suggest that the work has been done with perhaps a taste of relish as well as with devotion. All too obviously they come to reflect that preoccupation with violence of all sorts, sacred and secular, which is common to the two cultures, Spanish and Amerindian, which come together in Latin American life.

But all the statues of this sort had been taken for the processions. One small statue remained, poignantly forlorn and neglected. It was of Christ after His scourging. He sat alone in a corner, His head drooping, His face not only inexpressibly sad, but suggesting also the bewilderment of someone who momentarily at least believes He has been forsaken by both God and man. With chin on hand and elbow on knee, He looked like a whipped, deserted, smaller version of Rodin's *Thinker*. Here, indeed, was a man of sorrows and acquainted with grief. And the crowd had hidden, as it were, their faces from Him.

Outside, the crowds milled around, nibbling incessantly, thousands of people breaking their Good Friday fast as they had been doing since early morning. Above their heads colored balloons in curious and amusing shapes floated in the air.

By ten o'clock that night the streets were almost deserted except for the road sweepers busily clearing away tons of discarded paper wrappings, ice cream cartons, fruit peelings, empty bottles, burst balloons, and broken toys.

Christ bearing His giant cross had been carried through the city for hours on end in half a dozen different processions. So, too, had His weeping mother and many saints who most certainly had not been present at the Crucifixion. Now they were all back in their allotted places in the churches to which they belonged.

For one day Guatemala City had been a gala city. Good Friday had been the big, exciting day of the year for scores of thousands of people for whom most days were like most others. Competition to be among the float-bearers had been great. Particular honor was attached to the job on Good Friday. A proportion of those who had carried the floats had seemed to be either more self-important or else, on the other hand, more deeply devotional than those of the preceding days. To the majority of the people who made up the milling crowds it had, one felt, been part-devotion, part-entertainment.

For them it had been an exciting mixture of pageantry and piety. For the vendors of toys and tasty titbits it had been a field day. Over most of Latin America it had been a day of strange paradoxes and almost macabre contrasts.

On the previous day I had gone to see the processions at Antigua, way out in the hills behind Guatemala City. The Holy Week processions in Antigua, once the civil and ecclesiastical administrative center for the whole of Central America, have a longer tradition; and they are grander, more highly organized than those in Guatemala City, the new capital. Their fame has spread far.

U.S. tourists fly down by the hundreds to be in Antigua on Maundy Thursday and Good Friday. By now many of the local people who take part in the processions are clearly conscious that this is not only an act of devotion, but a major tourist attraction too. As such, Antigua has everything, with its cobbled streets and Spanish-colonial buildings. If some of the tourists who see the processions in such a setting think of them, and of Catholicism, as being quaint and colorful survivals of a bygone age, this is understandable.

Heading the Maundy Thursday processions were columns of Mestizos and Indians dressed as centurions in helmets and breast plates and carrying pikes. Other centurions held back the pressing crowds. All those who played any part in the first Holy Week, from Pontius Pilate to Judas Iscariot, plus a number of Old Testament characters and a great many saints from later periods, were represented in the procession that day.

As a group of women carrying a float came along, the Catholic politician who had taken me there said with great feeling, "See how the Passion of our Lord and the sorrow of His mother iron out the differences between the classes. Today the richest and the poorest in this city are all equals." I looked and observed that those who marched ahead of the heavy swaying floats, or spurred on their bearers, were the daughters of the rich. The women and girls who staggered along under the weight of the huge floats were sweating bare-footed Mestizos and Indians with careworn faces and broken nails.

In Guatemala City it had been easy to be shocked by the chattering holiday crowd through which sweating men in purple robes had carried a thorn-crowned figure with gaudy red blood running down His agonized face and tortured body, or the figure of His weeping broken-hearted mother wringing her hands in an attitude of total despair.

I would not pretend to know what, in fact, it had really meant to the bare-footed little Indians. Those men with their enigmatic, almost expressionless Mayan faces I saw setting out that night, followed by heavily laden wives trailing over-tired children, to return to the poverty, squalor, hardship, and monotony which is the stuff of their everyday lives.

Some Catholics from abroad, scandalized by the Holy Week celebrations in Guatemala and elsewhere in Latin America, demand that they should be suppressed by the ecclesiastical authorities.

Similar demands are made from time to time for the suppression of some of the celebrations which occur on village patronal feast days. These, all too frequently, are days when more children are conceived out of wedlock and more men are hopelessly, disgustingly drunk than on any other days of the year.

There are those who argue that the Holy Week processions and patronal feast day celebrations degrade religion. At the best they make it a mere spectacle and at the worst perpetuate superstition, keep animism alive, and degrade those who participate in them. But there are others who take a different view. One leading Vatican diplomat in Latin America with whom I discussed this matter, argued that, instead of suppressing them, the Church should penetrate them more deeply with Christian thought and Christian practice. This is all the people have, he argued. What they learn of their religion starts with such processions. The visiting layman sees the element of gala, of entertainment; he sees the drunkenness and learns of other scandals. What he is less likely to be aware of is that many confessions are made by people on these days who have not been near the sacraments for years, sometimes not since their First Communion.

Still less does the visiting layman who has seen the immorality see also the marriages that are put right after unmarried partners have gone to pray in the churches, and who have then got into conversation with priests as a consequence.

What is indisputable is that many illiterate Indians and Mestizos learn what little they know of the Scriptures from the processions, just as the mediaeval European peasant learned from the crude, often coarse, knock-about morality and mystery plays, or from lurid paintings on church walls.

It was these processions, and even the superstitious practices too, which kept the memory of Christianity alive
throughout Latin America's priestless years and despite all
that anti-clericals and atheists could do against the Church.
This is certainly true of Guatemala which, even by Latin
American standards, had more than its share of both priestless years and anti-clericals.

The hard fact which has to be understood is that the
checkered history of Guatemala has left its mark on the
Church. Its all too obvious shortcomings today must be
seen against the tangled story of yesterday. The Church
long ago became the object of hatred and contempt on the
part of a large section of the educated class. All too frequently it was unloved because those who were seen as its
representatives were themselves unlovable. Too frequently
in the past it neglected the poor; and it is not surprising,
therefore, that it lost some of its effective hold on sections
of the urban poor.

Perhaps the most damning thing which can now be said
against it is that the Church is still seen as part of Guatemala's oligarchy. This is a situation which is to be found in
varying degree in many Latin American countries, and in
every case it is harmful to the Church.

If anyone is going to have any understanding of any
Latin American country, he must begin with some understanding of the state of the Church. And if he is going to
understand the state of the Church, he must learn something of its history too.

I am astonished when I meet newspapermen, political
commentators, even people in embassies who have spent
years in Latin America, and who have still made no attempt

to understand the Catholic Church and Catholicism as it is taught and practiced there. For no serious assessment of countries in the whole sub-continent can leave the Church out of consideration. This applies no matter whether it be religious, political, or social analysis.

We may question the right of Latin American countries to call themselves Catholic at all. We may stress that too frequently Catholicism in this area of the world is nominal. We may even with justification question the propriety of including the population of Latin America in the world Catholic total almost as though Latin Americans were Catholic to a man. But the fact still remains that the strength or weakness of the Church, its presence or its partial absence, its influence or its failure to make any real impact today, the boldness or timidity of its leaders, their vision or their lack of vision, their pronouncements and their silences are all equally important to any understanding of the situation.

Loved or hated, followed adoringly and blindly, or abandoned contemptuously, the Church in Latin America must always be taken into account. For Catholicism has decisively influenced the history and culture of these nations, and it will assuredly help to shape their future. It has profoundly influenced the personality of each individual Latin American. Any discussion of present problems or possible future developments must include some frank and, if necessary, even brutal assessment both of its strength and its weakness.

ANIMISTS AND ANTI-CLERICALS

Antigua has something of the excitement and mystery of Pompeii about it, with the difference that, although the de-

tails of an earlier way of life are, as in Pompeii, to be seen
on all sides, this city which was also hit by great natural
disaster, is still lived in—and the pace and way of life are
still today very much what they were at the time of the
disaster.

After twice being nearly ruined by earthquakes, Antigua
ceased to be Guatemala's capital city. But its people did not
abandon it. Yet the ancient streets and buildings remain
largely untouched. Enough of the old Spanish colonial university, for instance, exists for it still to be used in the
original way. The same is true of whole streets of magnificent houses and many other buildings both civic and ecclesiastical. These include the cathedral, the construction
of which began in 1569. The building work was finished in
1690, and it was left a ruin by the earthquake of 1773.
Even so the parts which survived are still in use.

I first visited the cathedral on Maundy Thursday. As I
was about to leave, I saw a small group of Indians disappear
down some steep steps which led under the cathedral floor.
I followed them into a low-roofed, dark little crypt where
candles burned before a cross. They and their forefathers
had been lighting candles there for so long that the walls
and roof were blackened with soot. So, too, was the cross
before which the Indians now silently prayed.

A few minutes earlier they had been saying prayers before the crucifix in the ruined cathedral. Now they prayed
some special prayers before a special cross. For in this one,
they believed, dwelt a spirit to whom due honor must also
be paid.

Over lunch a priest told me that that same morning one
of his best lay catechists had gone straight from serving
Mass to lead a band of pilgrims to a figureless cross high up

in the hills. There he led them in prayer. It was not to the God whom the Spaniards had brought to them 500 years ago that he and the other Indians had prayed, but to the spirit of the mountain whose cult went back far into the past and who, they believed, dwelt within this part-pagan, part-Christian symbol.

In Guatemala as in other Latin American countries, and particularly those where Indians form a high percentage of the population, the popular religion is often a strange mixture of Christianity and superstition. It is a mixture which shades off easily and naturally into superstition alone.

In many parts of Guatemala the Indians have erected their own crosses on which there is no figure of Christ. These crosses are frequently placed in spots where a nature spirit is believed to dwell. Often, when mission priests have brought an Indian community to the point where they believe the people now to be Christianized, they ask them, in a strange reversal of the more normal procedure, to get rid of the crosses they possess so that these may be replaced by crucifixes to which there is attached no suspicion of animism.

Indians form some 53 per cent of Guatemala's population. They and the near-Indian Mestizos are naturally and deeply religious. About this there can be no doubt. Just how "Christian" they are varies from individual to individual and, in particular, from area to area. Most often their religion is a mixture of Christianity and animism. Sometimes Christianity appears to be the dominant element; sometimes it is animism and superstition.

This need not surprise or shock anyone who knows anything of the Indians' story or of the tragic history of religion in Latin America as a whole. When the main missionary

thrust stopped (because, to a scandalous extent, of the un-
seemly squabbles between Spain and Rome) the process of
evangelization had reached the stage where ancient beliefs
and superstitions had still only recently been "baptized."
It is as though the evangelization of, say, Britain or Germany had almost ceased, and the missionaries had been
withdrawn, at the time when tree worship and other pagan
practices had still only partially been taken over by Christianity, and while there was a two-way traffic between the
ancient paganism and the new religion.

The process of reversion to pagan practices which began
when the flow of missionary priests slowed down was almost
inevitable, particularly as the common people had not yet
begun to produce their own clergy. How could they, indeed,
when they were illiterate almost to a man and when, as
time went on, more and more of their educated rulers opposed with fierce hatred almost everything for which the
Church stood? The wonder is not that bizarre practices are
to be found in Central America, or that superstition is inextricably mixed with Christianity, but that so much of
Christianity has survived despite all that has been done
against it over the centuries.

An illiterate Indian in Guatemala may turn Good Friday into a gala day. He may try to get the best of both
worlds by praying first before a crucifix, then hurrying off
to placate the spirit who dwells in a cross. In the circumstances, this need hardly surprise us. More surprising, at
first glance, may be the behavior of some well-to-do Guate-
malans who are not illiterate and who are not Indians.

An educated man, product of a university and inordi-
nately proud of the few drops of Spanish blood which flow
in his veins, will take his 14-year-old son to a brothel be-

cause the boy is now about to become a man. Hiring a prostitute, the father will demonstrate what should be done, then have his young son do the same as he stands by instructing him. (In some other parts of Latin America the boy's mother may arrange for a prostitute to come to the family home on his fourteenth birthday, and it is she who will then do the instructing.)

I naturally find the behavior of the person whose education brings him, as it were, into the mainstream of Western Christian culture, more startling than that of the illiterate Indian. Yet both have their roots in Latin America's tangled history.

So, too, has the anti-clericalism which takes such extreme forms among Guatemala's student population. Each year, on the eve of Holy Week, the university students of Guatemala City stage a blasphemous and obscene parody of the procession in honor of Our Lady of Sorrows. As a consequence the Church authorities have felt obliged to move the date of the official commemoration of Our Lady of Sorrows over to Holy Saturday in order that still more scandal and confusion may be avoided.

OLD-TYPE CHRISTIAN POLITICIAN

"Vietcong—heroes! Gringos—assassins!" The slogan painted in huge white letters stood out boldly on a smooth rock face at the side of the mountain road between Guatemala City and Antigua.

"Illegal Communist activities?" I asked a politician.

"Probably, but not necessarily," he replied. "Most of our people feel strongly about the U.S. being in Vietnam. They say that if the North Americans can blunder into such situations in Asia, they are even more likely to do so here in Latin America which is so much nearer to them."

But this is really by the way. I was traveling to Antigua, not to discuss Left-wing slogans, but to find José García Bauer, doyen of Guatemala's congressmen. A politician and lawyer, José never stops working, or crusading either, and is equally active in Church affairs as in politics. José's crusades, some would say, really belong to the last century. They have little to do with the post-Vatican Council II period and so take little account of current ideas on the Catholic's rôle in a pluralistic society—and this, after all, is what Guatemala is today. Indeed, José works tirelessly to get Church and State back to the days when the bishop's word was law for one and all.

I had been looking for José García Bauer for two days, journeying backward and forward between Guatemala City and Antigua in the hope that I might catch him at one or the other, for he commutes between the two. When I found him, he was, very typically, attending Mass in the chapel of Antigua's local prison along with some 100 of the prisoners and their families. It was Maundy Thursday morning when, according to all the rules and rubrics, no Mass should be said. But José had urged that Mass should be celebrated in the prison at that time, since otherwise the prisoners would have no Mass. And that was enough!

He is a Franciscan tertiary who spends much time in the local friary. And so this restless politician, who will never take no for an answer, had got, not one, but three Franciscan priests along to the jail to do as he asked. When I joined him, I found him leading the responses, keeping the singing going, acting as Master of Ceremonies. Even so, he broke off, and thereby momentarily brought the Mass to a standstill, in order to find me a corner practically behind the altar.

Most of the jail, built by the Spaniards long ago, was, like most of Antigua's other public buildings, a ruin. But enough of it still stood to meet local needs. Mass over, José took me off to the friary for a rough and ready lunch with his Franciscan friends. Already, I was recalling in my own mind the day I had met the equally controversial, erratic, and deeply committed Catholic Mayor La Pira of Florence. On that occasion we had had lunch in a home for juvenile delinquents to which La Pira had come straight from the Benedictine cell where he was currently living. La Pira is a Catholic politician of the Left. José García Bauer, in so far as he fits into any category, is a man of the Right. Yet the two have much in common.

Both are regarded as saints by some people and as mad by others. Both are born crusaders who tend to see their every political move as being the expression of God's will because they have first prayed earnestly about it.

José could not have been more courteous or cooperative. He was willing to discuss with me his views on the Church, politics, Communism, the social problems of his own people, the Faith in Guatemala. The "discussion" was, in fact, a fascinating monologue which lasted many hours.

The Church, he insisted, was making encouraging headway in Guatemala. He did not deny its weaknesses, but these had to be seen against the background of the far greater weaknesses of the past. It had to be remembered that by the end of the nineteenth century there were only 28 priests in all Guatemala. In one diocese, which is in the care of the Franciscans, there were now fifteen parishes, each with its own priest. In that same diocese a few years ago there were only two priests.

I asked one of the Franciscans with whom we were lunching what the state of the people was when his order moved into the diocese. His answer was brief but graphic. "Baptized flesh, that was all."

José and his friends acknowledged that many of the people of Guatemala have largely forgotten what little their forefathers knew about Christianity. They pray before statues in church, but as likely as not they are praying to some spirit who is supposed to dwell in that statue. The sabbath which the Indians keep is based on the old pre-Spanish Mayan calendar. Christian lay leaders, José declared, were urgently needed among the Indians, but all too often the only ones who showed signs of leadership were their witch doctors or pagan prayer leaders.

Turning to politics, José García Bauer explained that, although he was known as a Christian politician, he was not a member of the Christian Democratic party. The C.D.'s were suspect in the eyes of the Catholic hierarchy who consider their party to be leftist. José enjoyed the confidence and support of his Church's leaders, and this was something which he believed to be valuable and necessary. He was currently engaged in a fight which he saw as being one for the Faith. The new constitution, which was promulgated on September 15, 1965, was at that time under discussion; and he was fighting, clause by clause, line by line, to have restored to the Church rights and privileges which were taken from it in 1871.

Elsewhere, such privileges in a pluralistic society in the twentieth century might be regarded as more of a liability than an asset. There are many Catholics who would feel little regret if they saw them go. But for José and those who supported him the cry was "Back to pre-1871."

In Guatemala, as in Mexico, the Church, on paper, has practically no privileges today. But over the years many have been restored on the basis of custom and usage, even though the constitution has remained unchanged. This has occurred without any head-on clash with the anti-clericals, free-thinkers, and other opponents of the Church.

To quote but one example of how this works in practice: for generations no priest was allowed inside Antigua's local jail, still less was Mass permitted to be said there. It was José himself who successfully fought behind the scenes to have this privilege restored.

Other Catholic politicians to whom I talked, doubted the wisdom of José's campaign. They doubted, too, whether the ecclesiastical leaders were doing the best thing in making themselves a pressure group for the restoration of outdated privileges. They feared that this might open old wounds, revive ancient fears and antagonisms, and from there lead on to a demand that the concessions which have been unofficially made to the Church in recent years be taken back again. Moreover, the military government which was introducing the new constitution was itself unconstitutional, having come to power as a result of a coup d'etat. If, in due course, that government should be thrown out, might not the constitution which it had fathered be thrown out too? Any rights and privileges which had been quietly won back for the Church might then be lost. So, too, might the greater official tolerance toward religion which had proved so helpful to the Church.

Critics of the hierarchy, who exist in considerable numbers among the country's educated Catholics, felt that this was one more example of the way in which the bishops' thinking was failing to keep up with the times. Whereas in many parts of the world the Church was trying to disentangle itself from any tie-up with the State, in Guatemala the reverse at that time appeared to be the case.

NEW-TYPE CHRISTIAN POLITICIAN

Of a very different type to José García Bauer was René Armando de León Schlotter, head of the nine-year-old Christian Democrat party. At the time when I talked to him in Guatemala City, his was the only opposition party permitted by the military government.

René is a quiet-spoken, earnest man. Under Guatemalan conditions, he told me, for a Christian Democrat party to succeed, it must be the organized spearhead of a broad popular movement based upon trade unions, cooperatives, credit unions, peasant leagues, and syndicates.

This meant that not only urban workers and intellectuals, but peasants, too, must be brought into democratic activity. From this it flowed that his party must activize and organize half-starved and, therefore, apathetic illiterates. So there must be adult education to lift them out of the conditions which degrade them. Thus the mere act of trying to organize them involved simultaneously attempting to better their lot.

Every Christian Democrat leader in Latin America, no matter how obscure he may have been in the past, had had his hopes raised by the Christian Democrats' victories in Chile. There Eduardo Frei was elected president in December, 1964, and then, at elections held a few months later, was given a parliament dominated by his own party and, therefore, willing to support him in what he was trying to do. This had the effect of leading men who formerly were seen by the public, and who saw themselves, as little more than leaders of a lost cause to suddenly become aware of new possibilities—even if their country was a few thousand miles away from Chile.

Only a matter of months ago, René de León Schlotter had seemed far more likely to achieve political martyrdom than high office. He lived on a political knife-edge with the ever-present possibility that he might be arrested or sent into exile. When I met him, an authoritarian military government was in power, a state of siege had been in existence for several weeks, and his position was still a precarious one. Even so, because of Eduardo Frei's victory at the polls in Chile, there now dangled before his eyes the hope that one day he too might become his country's President. He admitted this quite frankly, but he conceded that everything, or just about everything, turned on Frei's future success or failure.

The main points in his party's program were demands for agrarian reform, a redistribution of industrial profits by means of profit-sharing schemes, effective laws to guarantee the existence of trade unions and peasant leagues, and thorough-going tax reforms.

There could be little doubt that every one of these was in accord with the needs of the country. But they frightened the rich and scared a good many of the prudent, traditionalist leaders of the Church as well. Moreover, René de León Schlotter frightened them as a leader. He had of late espoused the idea that the only way to beat the Communists and their allies was by promising as complete a revolution as they did and by outbidding them on every reform for which they agitated.

Given free elections, good leadership, and the right to organize on equal terms with others, a Christian Democrat party might quickly be carried to power on the basis of a platform like this—provided that the peasants and workers could be made to understand it. But restrictions placed by the military government on political organization and on activity by any party which considered itself to be Left of center were such that even the smiling, naturally optimistic René hardly dared plan beyond tomorrow.

"We consider ourselves to be to the left of the Christian Democrats of Chile," he told me. "And we strongly disagree with the political policies of the Christian Democrat party of Brazil because it accepts the military government which has taken over there. We do not accept our military government. Even the worst that can happen in a democratic regime is better than the best in a military one."

Current trends almost anywhere in Latin America today suggest that a political party must be Left of center if it is going to depend upon democratic processes and still at the same time have any prospect of early success. It must demand and work for radical reform. Its declared aim must be the transformation of the entire social structure.

But anyone who makes this his aim, and bases his policies on it, needs to be a big man with exceptional qualities of leadership. If he is to lead his party to power, he must be able to work with others and delegate responsibility to them no matter how dynamic he may be. He must also be prudent enough to be able to win to his side, or else to neutralize, sincere but timid men among Church leaders and within the middle class, and tough enough to fight strongly entrenched vested interests. This calls for considerable personal qualities as well as political skill.

In countries which, like Guatemala, have suffered for years from military dictatorships and authoritarian rule, it is extraordinarily difficult for such qualities to be developed and for the necessary political experience to be gained by the democrats. The fact that Eduardo Frei in Chile, which has a more democratic history than most Latin American countries, possessed the necessary qualities and was able to bring his party to power, is not in itself sufficient to qualify Christian Democrat leaders in other Latin American countries for similar power. Unless events turn in his favor, René de León Schlotter probably still has a long hard road ahead of him.

COMMUNIST GUERILLAS

Guatemala, which is an extraordinarily beautiful country with magnificent mountains, is a land of perpetual spring. It comes near to being a land of perpetual political crisis too.

Six weeks before I arrived, the Peralta government had declared a state of siege which was still technically in force. There were armed police halfheartedly guarding bridges, aqueducts, and installations and usually one or two extra hanging around the United States embassy. Apart from these few visible signs that the government considered a state of emergency to exist, one was not normally conscious of siege conditions.

The reason given by the government for the state of siege was that the activities of Communist guerillas in the hills and of the terrorists in the cities made this necessary.

The incident which had led to its being imposed was an alleged attempt on the life of the President. The man who in fact got shot was not the President, but an unfortunate army sergeant. Rumor had it that he had been sent as a decoy along the route which the Communist guerillas had expected the President to take while the President himself went home by another way.

For several years, during visits to Southeast Asia, I had heard Radio Peking and Radio Hanoi recounting the activities of Guatemala's Communist guerillas. Members of the clandestine Communist organization in Sarawak, North Borneo, I knew, were encouraged in their own preparations for "the armed struggle" as they learned from their transistor radios what Communist guerillas were doing on the other side of the world.

The writings of some of the Guatemalan Communist leaders published in the world Communist press seemed to indicate that here were men who already knew quite a lot about guerilla warfare.

Even so, I had not expected to walk into a siege which was acknowledged by the government to be in response to Communist guerilla and terrorist activities. Not that a state of siege or martial law was likely to surprise anyone who is accustomed to traveling in Latin American countries. What made it surprising was that the Guatemalan government had for years been denying, and when it could not deny, had been playing down, the very existence of Communist guerillas of any sort. Now, after having publicly stated time after time that no guerillas existed, it had given as its reason for the state of siege the activities of those allegedly nonexistent guerillas.

There were cynical chuckles coming from many of the

more politically sophisticated among the people of Guatemala City who had little opportunity to engage in normal democratic activity and so tended to view the political scene as onlookers and outsiders rather than as participants.

Of all the possible forms and types of government one can find in Latin America or anywhere else, the one which is least likely to initiate action, produce social change, or successfully combat Communism is almost certainly a weak, divided, authoritarian administration in the hands of the Army.

A strong military government may, for the time being, get things done. Even an unsatisfactory democratic government may at least provide an outlet, a safety valve, for the protest of the poor. But a weak, self-perpetuating, caretaker government composed of military men who are amateur politicians, at loggerheads with each other and fumbling around for a way to govern the country, is just about the worst that one can have. It was this sort of government which Guatemala now had. Even the halfhearted state of siege, and the circumstances under which it was imposed, were so many evidences of its ineptitude.

The very existence of the government itself was, as it were, a continuing assertion of the idea that political problems may legitimately be solved by military means. This being so, it was in no position either to build up any respect for democracy or to be given a sympathetic hearing when it tried to persuade the public that others who harbored the same idea should be rejected out of hand.

Neither the public's respect for government nor their regard for Guatemalan attempts at democracy were likely to be increased by the events which marked the end of Peralta's military government in 1966. The new constitution, third in 20 years, was approved and promulgated before elections for president, vice-president and a new congress were held in March, 1966. The only civilian candidate for president was Dr. Mario Méndez Montenegro.

Six months before the elections were due to be held, however, Dr. Méndez was found dead in his home. He had been shot through the heart. His death was at first officially described as suicide, but the police later admitted that it was a case of murder. The *Partido Revolucionario* (Revolutionary Party) then chose his brother, Dr. Julio César Méndez Montenegro, as its candidate. With the support of the non-Communist Left, he was in due course made President. He assumed office against a background of threats of *coups* by military leaders who, in the name of public safety, used the existence of Communist guerilla bands to try to win support for one more military take-over. Dr. Méndez Montenegro began his four-year term of office on July 1, 1966, with democrats hoping for the best, but, on the basis of hard experience, prepared for the worst that the military might do.

Restless young students who accepted their rulers' idea that political problems may legitimately be resolved by military means, were clearly more attracted to colorful Communist and Left-wing guerillas than to those whom they contemptuously dismissed as a bunch of fat colonels engaged in defending the interests of their own class.

Traditionally Guatemala's students bring out their own special edition of a satirical paper to coincide with their blasphemous parody of the procession of Our Lady of Sorrows. The latest issue was circulating when I arrived. It had been produced clandestinely in, it was said, neighboring

Salvador, then smuggled over the border. It bore a bogus *nihil obstat* and *imprimatur*.

The paper was in itself striking proof of the way in which the authoritarian character of the regime provided the students with one more reason for revolt and so forced them in the direction of Communism. For, added to the customary rebellious anti-clericalism, blasphemy, and obscenity was editorial support for the Communist guerillas. Across the top of the front page was a strip cartoon which depicted a rosary linking two candles labeled "*Falangistas*" and "*Jesuitas*" and ending with something labeled "Yon." There was, too, a long poem about "*El Chino Yon*," and the name of Yon appeared on practically every page.

The Yon referred to is Yon Sosa, a leader of the Communist guerillas whose story is sufficiently romantic to appeal to any rebellious or idealistic youngster. His father, I was told, is a well-to-do Guatemalan-Chinese businessman; his mother is a Latin American. Yon was a regular army officer who was selected to go to the United States for special training in guerilla warfare and anti-insurgency techniques.

On his return to his homeland he was shocked by its dictatorial regime and by the situation within the army to which he belonged. He started among his fellow officers in 1960 a non-ideological, anti-corruption movement which became known as the "13th of November Movement." When they failed to bring about the reforms they demanded, Yon and his supporters, in February, 1962, following a well-established Latin American tradition, took to the hills. They had already been branded as mutineers; now they became guerillas.

Their guerilla band was in due course influenced by Communism, and Yon, along with some of his companions, became a Communist. They proceeded to purge their movement of those Right-wing officers who had been associated with the original protest and in due course it became a Peking- and Cuba-orientated revolutionary army. Other Communist and Left-wing guerilla bands, usually composed of students, some urban workers, and a few peasants, have since linked up with them. Together they now form a small, well-led, efficient guerilla movement.

There are probably, all told, no more than 300 hard-core guerilla fighters permanently in the Guatemalan jungle. But to these must be added larger numbers of part-time guerillas, most often students, who go to the jungle bases for weekend and occasional training. There is also an urban, mainly working-class, terrorist organization.

Some of the leaders received their training in guerilla warfare and terrorism in Cuba, others in China. The jungle-covered mountains in which the guerilla bands operate are ideal for guerilla activity. The largest concentration of guerillas is in the hills close to a highway linking the capital with the country's main Atlantic port where they have their principal city base.

Not long before my arrival in Guatemala, insurgents seized a small garrison town and held it for long enough to demonstrate to the local populace that it was not the army and government who controlled the situation there, but the guerillas. The guerillas helped themselves to the garrison's arms before pulling out.

Confronted with the threat of serious guerilla activity, the army's first response was to use rough methods. Hundreds of innocent people in the affected areas were arrested and kept in jail without trial for months on end. Villages, thought to be sympathetic to the insurgents, were raided, and homes burned down. These actions were frequently accompanied by raping and looting, and this led to a growth of resentment among the people. Predictably, they helped only the Communists.

Then the Army, attempting to create a new image of itself, switched to trying to make friends with the people, by taking them food and medicine, delivering babies, introducing a Civic Action Program, and initiating small agrarian and other reforms. But the earlier, repressive measures had enabled the Communists to gain that local popular support—or neutrality—which guerillas must have before they can establish the essential support bases.

The fact that the Army's Civic Action Program is confined to areas where sympathy for the rebellion is known to exist is not lost on the people. They do not have to be very wide-awake to know that the best thing that can happen to them is that a guerilla band should start to operate somewhere not too far away.

The illegal, Moscow-orientated Guatemalan Party of Labor (*Partido Guatemalteco del Trabajo*—"P.G.T."), as the Communist party has called itself since 1952, has for the past dozen years or so maintained its membership at around 1,000. Its main support comes from students, urban workers, and middle-class intellectuals.

The position of a Moscow-line Communist party in a country in which there is a Left-wing guerilla movement is today a difficult one. The type of man who becomes a Communist will almost inevitably be attracted to Left-inspired armed struggle. Moscow's own inclination has traditionally been to back trouble anywhere, and the Russian leaders undoubtedly welcome any movement which could someday provide an opportunity to establish a Communist base in the Western hemisphere. For these reasons, despite all its talk of peaceful roads to socialism, Moscow gives encouragement to the Communist guerillas, and Guatemala's Moscow-orientated Communists support the insurrectionary movement.

Hugo Barrios Klee, a Communist leader in exile, writing in World Marxist Review (Problems of Peace and Socialism) in September, 1964, said:

"In the present situation the character of the struggle and scale of its impact on the masses should be decisive when choosing the form of struggle (provided there is a choice). Should the switch to armed struggle isolate the vanguard from the masses and reduce their political activity, the result would be a slowing down of the revolution.

"The experience of revolutions shows that the transition to armed action brings success only when it is supported by the masses, when it is linked with their daily struggle and stimulates this struggle.

"We believe that these conditions exist in Guatemala. Our Party therefore supports the guerilla actions now taking place in the country. . . .

"Flaring up anew after the March coup, guerilla warfare is now the main form of the democratic struggle. Guerilla units actively support the resistance movement in the towns and rural areas where armed action is the answer to repressions. The success of the guerilla movement in the northeast, the participation of farm laborers and peasants in it, the beginnings in the south of an armed struggle having a similar social base, are signs of the progress being made in forming a revolutionary army. These guerilla actions will

gradually become more and more organized and consistent.
By striking at the regime's machinery of violence, they will
thereby help to smash it. . . ."

Moscow and its followers must, however, also give some
appearance of reality to their talk and the possibility of
using "constitutional struggle" today and to the international policy of peaceful coexistence. So Guatemala's "official" Communists have also to declare somewhat halfheartedly and unconvincingly that there may just possibly,
given other circumstances, be some chance of bringing
about the revolution by non-violent processes. This puts
them at a disadvantage with other Communists and Left-
ists.

The initiative for the "13th of November Movement"
did not come from the Moscow-Communist P.G.T. Many
of the guerillas owe their allegiance, not to Moscow, but to
China, or are inspired by Cuba. The P.G.T. publicly supports the guerillas, and there can be no doubt that within
the hard core of the guerilla movement it has its members
and supporters. But because it is inhibited by the contra-
dictions in the Moscow line, and because of the tensions
and divisions in the world Communist movement, it does
not work as closely with others as the situation demands.
This can have the effect of weakening the armed movement
as a whole. But, conversely, it also tends to drive the more
militant elements among the Communists and their sym-
pathizers into greater support for Peking whose approach
to the armed struggle is unequivocal and uninhibited.
Given a worsening economic situation or yet one more
political crisis, the guerillas could become a serious threat
to Guatemala.

The very existence of the guerillas and the insistence by

Communist leaders of both the Moscow and Peking camps that "guerilla warfare is now the main form of the democratic struggle" in Guatemala makes it immensely more difficult for democracy to function. Military and political leaders of the extreme Right who are eager to defend the power of the old ruling groups use the Communist threat against their more liberal opponents.

When the military government in December, 1965, announced that it had uncovered a widespread Communist plot to seize power, democrats saw this as an attempt to create a panic atmosphere as a prelude to the presidential elections. It is possible that the Communists, for their own reasons, wished to prevent the elections and therefore intensified their campaign of terrorism and sabotage. But the non-Communist Left could be forgiven for supposing that the government's revelations were intended as propaganda against themselves.

What I found particularly disturbing was that both the local rich and American circles in Guatemala seemed to take it for granted that, if things should someday get seriously out of hand, with a genuine danger of the guerillas taking over, the United States could be relied upon to intervene, just as it had done in 1954.

Whatever the consequences of such intervention might be in Guatemala itself, there is little doubt that it would help the cause of Communism all over Latin America and, for that matter, in Asia and Africa too. If Communists could pray, they would surely ask that there should be, somewhere in Latin America, a military takeover every few years and, ideally, alternating with this, that America should either send in the Marines or put in some corrupt puppet-dictator somewhere else.

The Communists of Guatemala have been aided, not only by the succession of *coups d'etat*, assassinations, and military juntas which have formed the pattern of political life throughout the post-war years, but by the failure on the part of almost everyone concerned to do anything significant about urgently needed social reforms.

The Catholics have been the most vocal opponents of Communism, but it is anyone's guess whether those who have denounced Communism most loudly have strengthened or weakened it by doing so. They have not in any case usually been among the most outspoken champions of social justice. Because of the identification of the Church with the oligarchy, Catholic opposition to Communism has been made suspect among the people. Many still feel that, although some of the Catholic anti-Communist campaigners have opposed it for its atheism, far more have done so because it threatens their own wealth and privileges.

Sometimes the cause of Communism in Guatemala has been aided by churchmen who thought in terms which were hard to justify in the nineteenth century and are even harder to defend today. In the early post-war years, when there was the genuine possibility of a Communist take-over, there were prominent churchmen who were still insisting that liberals and Masons were even more dangerous than Communists. Their sweeping condemnation even included liberals who were regular Mass-goers. Many of those so denounced were known to the common people who could not, try as they would, see them as sinister. They not unnaturally concluded that, if the Communists were *less* bad than these, then there was not much to be said against Communism.

Although the country's needs are more urgent than

most, there is probably as little positive, Church-inspired work for socio-economic betterment in Guatemala as anywhere in Latin America. Much of what social activity can be credited to the Church has been initiated by foreign priests who have not always had the support of members of the local hierarchy.

The little people of the Guatemalan countryside, particularly the Indians, still have little cause to feel that they really matter to those who rule them. The young people of the towns are frustrated by the restrictions on democracy, the constant intervention of the military in political affairs, the resistance to social change by those who control the levers of power, and the knowledge that, although their country may be politically independent, it remains economically dependent upon a United States which still tends to treat it as its puppet.

There can be little doubt that many of the people who join or support the guerillas do so in the belief that the domestic and foreign forces of reaction which control the destiny of their country are so determined to block all real reform that only revolution is left to them. They see the Church as being on the side of the *status quo*, identified with a ruling class which is determined to concede as little as possible either in the way of democratic rights or social justice.

Members of the Peace Corps may come from the United States and start excellent projects here and there, but the memory of past interventions and the possibility of future ones tend to make their task more difficult.

United States government-sponsored aid programs provide evidence that there are Americans in high places who have a genuine desire to help their impoverished neighbors.

But the Latin American understandably wants to be treated as an equal and so approaches even this with caution.

Egypt's former Finance Minister Abdul Galil al-Emary once compared his country's economy with a huge cow that grazed on Egyptian pastures while its udders were being milked in foreign lands. Central America still has its udders in the United States and so, with all the goodwill in the world, Americans working on aid projects encounter difficulties when they seek to convince the people of the genuineness of their intentions.

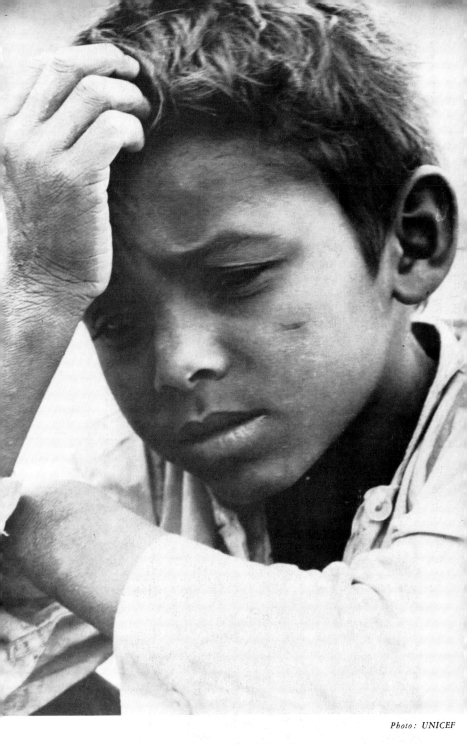

Photo: UNICEF

A small Venezuelan boy from a large family bears not only
his burdens but those of his brothers and sisters also.

Photo: Bolivia Alianza

Agricultural techniques being developed in Bolivia under the Alliance for Progress.

Village girls in Patzun, Guatemala, use long bamboo poles to conduct water from the fountain to their jars. Whitewashed church in the background dates back to the Spanish colonial period.

Oregon Peace Corps worker, Doug Brown, with a family in the village of La Concepcion outside Panama City.

Students and police clash in open rioting in Caracas, Venezuela.

Anti-government guerillas in the Falcon Mountains in Venezuela.

Another Cuba That Wasn't

3

The word *another* has in recent years acquired an emotional quality which now influences the public's thinking and even some governments' policies. It has only to be invoked to reduce a section of the public to a condition in which thought ceases, emotion takes over, and almost any drastic action, no matter how little justified, becomes acceptable. Each of the three developing continents has its *another* land. Africa has its Congo; Asia, its Vietnam (and Korea); Latin America and, indeed, the whole Western Hemisphere, its Cuba.

Say that there is a danger that Laos, Cambodia, or Malaysia may become "another Vietnam," and everyone is prepared for the worst. The line that Rhodesia may become "another Congo" brings together moderates and racists among the white population in a mood of self-protectiveness. To talk in the United States of "another Cuba" is enough to put some sections of the public in a state of mind where they are prepared to see the Marines go into action at once.

Nothing but this *another* psychosis could surely explain

the degree of excitement created by the incident which occurred in Panama in January, 1964.

This incident was recalled for me by an announcement
made by a stewardess on my flight from Guatemala to Panama. She told us that we were now approaching Panama
City and then went on to state that the Panamanian government wanted to stress that United States citizens were
particularly welcome. Those of us on board who were not
U.S. citizens felt suitably cut down to size. Here, indeed,
it seemed, was the dollar talking in accents loud, clear, and
unmistakable.

Then I reflected that this was intended to reassure
American visitors who might understandably be fearful of
the reception they might get in Panama. It was an attempt
to undo, at the tourist level, the consequences of the earlier
events.

The origins of the trouble, which began on January 4,
1964, could hardly have been smaller or, in the exact meaning of the word, more childish. As President Johnson was
later to declare, there were "excesses and errors on the part
of both Americans and Panamanians." It started when, in
December, 1963, the Governor of the Panama Canal Zone
—that survival of an earlier period which cuts Central
America into two pieces with a little strip of U.S. territory
between them—announced that the Panamanian and U.S.
flags would no longer fly together outside schools in the
Canal Zone. The Stars and Stripes would, however, continue to be displayed inside the schools.

Flags happen to mean a lot in countries where nationalism is still in the ascendancy. They also mean much more
in the United States than in most European countries today. So in due course some U.S. high school boys in Balboa,

in the Canal Zone, in defiance of the Governor's order, ran up the Stars and Stripes outside their school. A handful of Panamanian students, who happened to feel strongly about flags, responded in kind by marching from their own part of the country into Balboa and putting their flag beside the American one, outside the high school.

"Actions of imprudent students from both countries," President Johnson said, "played into the hands of agitators seeking to divide us." Significantly, the President, unlike some American commentators, was careful not to attach any particular label to those "agitators." Nationalism needs little in the way of agitation to make it boil over at the best of times, and when it exists against the background of a desire on the part of a small nation to get a better deal from a big and powerful one, big events may have very small beginnings.

Be that as it may, there followed riots, which spread from the Canal Zone into the Republic of Panama. Before they were through, four American servicemen and some 20 Panamanian civilians had been killed; other casualties totaled several hundreds. The U.S. Embassy in Panama City was evacuated because of "threatening crowds," and the U.S.I.S. building was burned down.

The matter went to the U.N. Security Council and to the O.A.S. Peace Committee. Diplomatic relations were broken off by Panama "in view of American acts of aggression." They were not restored until April 4, by which time Panama's demand that the Canal treaties should be revised had been satisfied. By then, too, both national flags were flying outside the Canal Zone schools once more.

But long before the riots were over, the incident was being represented in some quarters as an attempt at a Communist take-over. Panama, it was alleged, was in danger of becoming *another* Cuba. The most up-to-date figure for the membership of the Communist party of Panama, that for 1963, was just 150. It goes without saying that Peking took up the Panamanian cause with enthusiasm. Twelve months later the *Peking Review* had still not stopped trying to exploit it to the full and to use it as a stick with which to beat America.

The situation produced no Panamanian Fidel Castro, least of all from among the agitators to whom President Johnson had referred. All in all, the situation could hardly have been less like the one in which the Cuban leader toppled Batista's inhuman dictatorship with the last-minute support of a Communist party big enough, and experienced enough, to later decisively influence the whole course of the revolution.

By the spring of 1965, the political temperature had dropped. As the statement by the airline stewardess made embarrassingly obvious, the Panamanian government had by then clearly decided that it was not going to let the riots of 1964, nor the desire for a new Canal Zone treaty, interfere with the flow of dollar-laden American tourists to its territory. Panama self-evidently was not another Cuba.

Only a little later that same spring of 1965, the American government and public were persuaded that there might be another Cuba in the offing. This time it was the Dominican Republic. The U.S. Government had at that moment good reason to know from its increasing involvement in Vietnam that interventions in other countries' domestic squabbles can become big and costly affairs. It seems, therefore, momentarily at least to have believed reports that this might be another Cuba. The Marines were sent in. The violence in Santo Domingo proved to be on a far larger scale than that in Panama. But by the time the Marines had been pulled out again, the administration had become convinced that its original advice was misconceived. This knowledge had, I fear, been obtained at the cost of much valuable goodwill.

The Dominican Communist party must have felt somewhat wistful as it heard all the talk of the possibility of an imminent Communist take-over. For this little party provides grim evidence that a dictator who is willing to use repression and terrorism without regard for human life or human rights can come near to physically eliminating every Communist in the land. The Communist party had tried to oppose the Trujillo tyranny. By the time Trujillo fell, only a handful of exiles remained. These returned to the Dominican Republic, but the Communists had neither the leaders nor had they had the time to rebuild their forces when the Marines went in to put down another Cuba.

The Christian Democratic Challenge

4

We have seen from the case of Guatemala that Christian Democrats who had hardly dared to let themselves think of success at any time in the foreseeable future suddenly had their hopes raised by Eduardo Frei's success at the polls in Chile.

Not all those who began to think in terms of the possibility of soon becoming other Freis were necessarily of his stature. Nor were their parties ready for power, even if it should come their way. But that was not true in the case of Venezuela.

Venezuela's Christian Democrats are, by any standards, and certainly by those of Latin America, fit for power. Before long they may be ready for it too. It is not difficult to visualize their leader, Dr. Rafael Caldera, as his country's president, for he stands out as one of Latin America's most impressive politicians, impressive for his personality, his political maturity, and his integrity.

This humane, intelligent, and serious-minded man is not concerned with such labels as "Left" and "Right." He has had both attached to him at one time or other, sometimes simultaneously. Nor does he gibe at the use of the word *revolution*. Peaceful social revolution, he insists, is his country's urgent need. He sees this revolution, not as an end in itself, but as growing naturally out of his country's history and the situation in which Venezuela finds itself today. The fact that he is for peaceful, not violent revolution, makes him no less a revolutionary, for he is deeply convinced of the need for the total transformation of the social structure.

Dr. Caldera feels a close sense of political kinship with Eduardo Frei, although Frei probably stands somewhat to the Left of him in practice. There are, he says, obvious differences between Venezuela and Chile. Castro's Cuba is close to Venezuela. It is two days' journey from Chile. This means that Fidel's impact on Venezuela has been far greater than on Chile, although even there, the fear of Chile's becoming "another Cuba" undoubtedly influenced people who were to the right of Frei to vote for him rather than split the anti-Communist vote.

"We Christian Democrats are all convinced," Dr. Caldera told me in his office in Caracas, "that a revolution is necessary in Latin America. We are not just accepting it, we are promoting it." Germany, he went on, was seen as a capitalist stronghold. Yet far more of Germany's budget was allocated to social security than was the case in Venezuela. Here, he said, a minister has 2,500 dollars a month. At the other end of the social scale, down at the lowest rung, there are people who have 100 dollars a year.

He is not surprised that some of the poor in this "Catholic" country are influenced by Communist and other Marxist propagandists. He describes them as "red fishes swimming in blessed water." The vast majority of our people, he says, are left of center. And this must necessarily be reflected in the policies and thinking of a party which calls itself, not only Christian, but democratic too.

The left-ward thinking he attributes in part to the fact that a large proportion of the population is young. This, incidentally, has validity, not only for Venezuela, but for a great many other developing countries with fast-growing populations where the same political trend is apparent. It is, for example, as meaningful for Singapore as for Venezuela.

Young people, Dr. Caldera says understandingly, desire change, and they want it quickly. Therefore the trend is for change.

He holds that Venezuela offers special opportunities to a Christian Democracy which reflects at one and the same time the people's traditional Christianity and the desire for democratic change. There is a political vacuum to be filled. The Conservative party was defeated a century ago by the Liberal party, and since then no one has dared to call himself Conservative. In the period that followed, Venezuelan Liberals, like those in some other Latin American countries, often supported a particular family and kept them in power. Then the Venezuelan Liberal party was destroyed by dictators. In time the public wearied of dictators, so that by now conservatives, liberals, and dictators are alike discredited.

"We are defenders of traditional institutions, but we support a change of structure," says Dr. Caldera. "The Conservatives want to keep the structure; the Communists are against both. We want to change the structure in order to suffuse the old institutions with a new sense of freedom. We wish to strengthen such fundamental institutions as the family, the Church, State, the economy, social organizations, and the trade unions in accord with the new desire for freedom."

As in Guatemala, but with far greater success, the Christian Democrat party has become the center of a movement which extends much beyond the party itself. For example, Christian workers have their own trade unions, but they also work within the non-sectarian ones. There had, said Dr. Caldera, been an unexpected trend toward Christian democracy in the unions. Followers of his party had recently won union elections in a metal factory, then in two iron mines, and then in the local Ford factory. Members of *Acción Democrática*, the ruling party, were by now openly fearful that the Christian Democrats would soon have the industrial leadership of the oil industry too.

The strength of the Communists has for years been confined to certain small sectors of industry. In contrast, the Christian Democrats are branching out into new fields. The largest group of unions, for the time being at least, remains linked with the Latin American wing of the U.S.-dominated International Confederation of Free Trade Unions, but there is now a movement away from the I.C.F.T.U. to specifically Christian trade unions.

Confidently, Dr. Caldera told me that the Christian Democrats were "optimistic that we may get the people's endorsement of our development program for Venezuela at the next elections."

In thinking of such development, he is not concerned only with economics. An economic development which makes the rich richer, but leaves the gap between rich and poor still as great as ever, would not satisfy him. If the development is to be truly Christian, it must be one which ensures that the whole of the population shares in any new prosperity.

For a developing country, in particular, there can be no significant social change without a strong economic base, and this would therefore be the Christian Democrats' first aim. But even while this is being built, it would be their aim also to foster greater participation in the productive effort by the people themselves.

The Christian Democrats refuse to accept the present situation, in which out of a working population of approximately three million, some one-tenth of these are unemployed. Here is a problem which confronts many another country at the same stage of development as Venezuela. On the one hand there are large numbers of unemployed; on the other hand, there is a chronic lack of skilled workers. This, says Dr. Caldera, is absurd.

The present progress of technical education, which should be the deciding factor in reducing the number of unemployed while increasing the number of skilled workers, would not solve the problem in 100 years. The whole pace of progress in technical education has to be immensely accelerated. "We want," he told me, "to make people feel that they are building a new country—the sort of feeling that they have, for example, in Israel."

One thing that augurs well for the Christian Democrats' future is that they control the largest of the student associations in the universities and that these attract some of the best among the country's students. They have some of the most promising young leaders, including ones who, it is claimed, may well prove to be as brilliant as Dr. Caldera himself. Their boast is, too, that their party is now attracting some of the best brains in the land. One man in a position of great influence in the life of Caracas told me: "If we need a group of doctors, engineers, specialists, technicians, or professional men to advise or assist us, it is to the Christian Democrats that we must go."

The new Latin American Christian Democracy, of which that in Venezuela is a good example, aims at something more than being composed of a confessional party and confessional trade unions. In its concern for moral and ethical values, and for protecting the rights of the human person, it is essentially Christian. But it does not confine its appeal to Christians.

It sets out to appeal to anyone who wishes to see political, economic, and social progress achieved within the framework of democracy. It rejects absolutely that disregard for the individual's rights which has been a feature of so many of the dictatorships and military governments that have been part of Latin America's history in general and that of Venezuela in particular.

DEMOCRACY UNDER DIFFICULTIES

When a popular revolt toppled the bloody dictatorship of Pérez Jiménez in 1958, the Christian Democrats went into President Rómulo Betancourt's government. They refused, however, to go into the coalition, headed by President Raúl Leoni, which followed it.

Probably no Latin American country has had, until very recent years, a more turbulent political history than Venezuela, with one government after another overthrown by the military, and with a sorry succession of dictators notorious for their bloody suppression of any attempt at opposition. It is estimated that Venezuela has had around 50 revolutions since it gained its independence in 1810. (Bolivia has had 150.) When the Betancourt government actually survived its full term of office, this was something new in the country's history. To the last, no one could believe that it, or any other democratic government, could actually run its full course.

Once, long ago, Betancourt was a Communist. By the time I met him in 1961 he was one of Latin America's most intelligent anti-Communists. He was quietly but firmly dealing with Communist subversion, while at the same time trying to achieve, by means of ambitious land reform and other projects, at least the beginnings of the process of attacking the social causes of Communism. Even so, I found many wealthy people in political and religious circles who were prepared to keep the whisper going that "perhaps he is still a Communist" and that, therefore, it was time that the military should step in and take over the government once more.

With a background such as this, a democratic government must be strong if it is going to survive in Venezuela's political jungle. Genuine democrats I met during my latest visit were fearful lest the all too evident weakness of the Leoni government should lead to yet one more military coup. Within one month of Leoni's election, members of the class from which dictators and military juntas have traditionally been drawn were already saying: "Who knows, we may have to get the military in again."

The uncertainty and the timidity of the government led also to a public questioning of its good faith. Weakness in Latin America leads to the growth of corruption. This operates at two levels. First, there is that of the common people. They are in the hands of officials who take petty bribes as their due—such as the accepted custom of wrapping up a request for a motor license in a small bundle of notes. But there is the second form of corruption which is less blatant, but probably more harmful to the morale of the common people. This takes the form of the rich getting what they want done through family connections. As one Venezuelan of this class put it to me. "This is a country of whom you know, not what you know."

This is, as it were, a hangover from the past, a feudal survival in an increasingly industrial society. Working against it is the emergence of a small but growing class of men with new businesses, who own small factories, or who head various industrial agencies. They live in moderately luxurious homes, usually obtained with a big mortgage. On every count they are on the side of stability. They have a vested interest in it and are prepared to work for it. This new middle class is likely to be of increasing importance in the country's life.

The fact in any case is that in the elections of 1963 one constitutional president was chosen to succeed another— for the first time ever.

EMERGENT CHRISTIAN TRADE UNIONS

A growing number of industrial workers for one reason or another reject the Communists, yet are not entirely satisfied with those unions which look to North America for their inspiration. For these the Christian trade unions have a growing appeal.

As is the case in most Latin American countries, trade unions in Venezuela may be linked with any one of three groups, each with its international connections, although a number remain unattached. There are those which are linked with ORIT, which is the Latin American section of the International Confederation of Free Trade Unions. This is usually the largest group.

Then there are those which are Communist-controlled or Communist-influenced. These usually have some links with the World Federation of Trade Unions which is itself Communist-controlled. Support for the Communist unions in most Latin American countries is waning today, and W.F.T.U. as an organized force within Latin America has declined almost to a point of non-existence. In the early years after World War II it had its own very active centers in Latin America. It was easy to suppose that before long it might become the dominant force from the northern-most tip of Central America to the southernmost tip of South America. But during the period of the cold war it ceased to make headway, then lost its hold in one country after another. There are still some Communist-dominated and Marxist unions which have a considerable following, but the majority of these appear to have no continuous contact with W.F.T.U.

A third group consists of the Christian trade unions. Most, though not all of these, are linked with CLASC (*Confederación Latinoamericana de Sindicalistas Cristianos*), which is the Latin American section of the International Federation of Christian Trade Unions. In most countries these unions, though still small, are growing at the expense of both the ORIT and Communist-affiliated unions. Again, in most, though not all, they are formally linked with Christian Democrat parties or feel themselves to be part of the industrial wing of a movement which is Christian Democratic in aim and outlook.

In Venezuela, those linked with ORIT form the largest group, organizing some 65 per cent of all trade unionists. The second largest consists of those unattached unions which are neither "Christian" nor ORIT. Most of these are in fact Communist-controlled, although the majority of their members are most certainly not Communists. They are either workers who have no desire to be linked with a body which is regarded as Yankee-influenced or are ones who, being in the Latin American anti-clerical tradition, fight shy of anything which calls itself Christian.

The Christian group, as might be expected, consists of unions the majority of whose members feel themselves to be Christians—although there are some unions in which the Christian influence is strongest and which nonetheless belong to the ORIT group. Thus the number of "Christian" unions cannot be judged by how many are affiliated with CLASC; still less can the number of Christians in Venezuela's unions be judged by the total membership of the CLASC-affiliated unions.

Typically Latin American (although one may find a similar situation in the Philippines, where the same Spanish tradition is to be found) is the fact that most of the specifically Christian trade unions owed their initial inspiration to priests. Priests helped with their formation, saw them launched, and then, when they were well under way, pulled out, and before long they were doing the same again with some other group of workers. Many of those workers who are joining Christian unions today are of the type who in the past would have had no truck with anything bearing a Christian label.

Father Aguala, a Spanish Jesuit who has been the moving spirit behind the formation of many of Venezuela's

Christian unions, told me that a growing proportion of their recruits are men with long trade union experience who have become disenchanted with Marxism.

The Latin American tradition has been for the average union leader to be more concerned with using his union as a stepping-stone to a political career than with the betterment of the lot of his members. Probably the movement's greatest need—and this goes for much of Latin America—is, therefore, for trained, dedicated leaders who understand what should be the true rôle of a union and who are qualified to run an organization in an efficient and businesslike way.

To meet this need, Father Aguala now devotes almost all his time to organizing courses in trade union procedure and in the history, principles, and philosophy of trade unionism.

I asked Father Aguala why he considered it necessary to create yet one more group of unions, thus dividing the workers still further, when there are already the "democratic" and the "Communist" unions which between them should surely cater to all. His answer was one which, to the visitor unfamiliar with Latin America, may sound unconvincing the first time it is heard. But I have heard it, or something like it, repeated over and over again in every part of Latin America by priests and laymen, by hardheaded Christian Democrat politicians and equally hardheaded trade union leaders. The more one knows about Latin America, the more one is prepared to accept its validity.

It goes like this: the American dominated ORIT unions tend to reflect a materialistic North American philosophy of life. In other words, U.S. trade unions are primarily, and

CHRISTIAN DEMOCRATIC CHALLENGE 63

frequently exclusively, concerned with improving their members' material conditions. Their concern is only with such matters as hours of labor and working conditions. This concept of the rôle of the trade union has an initial attraction for the impoverished Latin American worker, but then, as its narrow materialism becomes more apparent, it begins to jar. It clashes with "the spirit of Latin America;" it lacks a "mystique."

The U.S. unions are the products of a society which has achieved an unprecedented degree of material affluence, but which, in Latin American eyes, has paid the price for this in cultural and spiritual poverty. Latin Americans, it is argued, are at least as concerned with ideas as with material things, and any philosophy or approach to life which leaves this out of account must necessarily fail to satisfy them.

If the U.S.-orientated ORIT unions are too materialistic in their outlook for Latin American tastes, this is true also of those which are Moscow-orientated, though in a different way. The great advantage that the Marxist unions had over the "democratic" ones, when Latin American workers first, in the post-war years, felt the impact of W.F.T.U., was that the Communists appeared to be idealists, while the Americans were materialists.

Then, during the cold war period, they came to learn more about Marxism and to know something of its materialistic philosophy. Once they realized that this was incompatible with the things of the spirit, many of them shied away from it. The process of disenchantment was repeated among new groups of workers when Castro came to power and then in due course began, like Moscow, to lose something of his appeal.

Christian trade unionists argue that neither ORIT nor

W.F.T.U. adequately reflects the Latin American spirit. By basing themselves on ideas, beliefs, and principles, the Christian unions meet a need which neither of the others can hope to satisfy.

This may all sound very up-in-the-clouds to a hard-headed trade unionist from North America or Europe. But it makes good sense in Latin America. The proof of the pudding is in the eating. Christian trade unions in Venezuela, and throughout much of Latin America, are undoubtedly at this moment attracting workers for whom the other two international bodies never at any time had an appeal. They are also attracting some of the people who have been disenchanted by either ORIT or W.F.T.U. And, strangely enough for the outside, many of this latter group really have left ORIT or W.F.T.U. unions because they have found their materialism unacceptable.

As often obtains in areas where there is no long history of democracy and where the mass of the working people are still below the poverty line, trade unions have "supporters" rather than members. Only in a very few places has the idea, familiar enough in North America and in Europe, got across that you join a union, pay a regular contribution to its funds, and have continuing membership and loyalty to it over the years. Latin American workers normally only start paying membership dues to a union when either a wage claim or a dispute is in sight. Once the immediate objective has been achieved, they may continue to support the union and to follow the lead given by those at the top, but it does not occur to them to continue to pay dues.

One effect of this is that hardly any of the leaders rise from the ranks. The overwhelming majority have had no experience of industrial life. They are of the middle class, usually professional men, and very frequently men who are thinking in terms of a political career. These see union leadership as providing them with a position of power from which they can bargain their way into the leadership of a particular party.

Another effect is that, if a leader is going to continue to hold his members and keep his organization in existence at all, he must be constantly involved in wage claims and disputes—and must be able to show results. "Buying" leaders becomes all too easy, and both ORIT and W.F.T.U. are charged with doing precisely this.

CLASC sets itself firmly against this tradition. Admittedly, it may not be able to persuade poverty-stricken and half-starved campesinos regularly to pay their membership dues to a peasant union. But by basing their activities on Christian principles which have a permanent validity in the lives of their followers, the Christian unions nevertheless achieve some sort of continuity of support. In Peru, to take a case in point, the CLASC peasant unions can probably claim very few regular dues-paying members, but there can be no doubt that their influence is a rapidly growing one in the rural areas. The supporters grow in numbers, but they simply cannot afford to be members.

It was natural that when trade unionism first began to spread in Latin America, it should model itself on movements which already existed in other parts of the world and so affiliate with them. Its concepts, like much else in Latin America, were "borrowed." But today Latin Americans are increasingly eager to evolve in a truly Latin American way. If this process continues, then the future may very well be much more with the Christian unions than with the others.

CAMPUS POLITICS

Latin America's students are some of the most politi-cally-minded on earth. But that needs qualifying. It may be more accurate to say that they are probably the most deeply involved in political activity and are more shamelessly used by political parties than anywhere.

Hack politicians are forever busy on the campus, on the lookout for any student who can be used for the narrowest party ends. Feelings run high about the contending claims of the rival conventional parties, but it is doubtful whether political thinking by their supporters necessarily goes very deep. Only in the Left-wing groups which abound on every campus is there usually serious discussion of genuinely im-portant political issues. This, of course, adds to the attrac-tion of the Left. Those attracted tend, inevitably in the cir-cumstances, to be the more sensitive and intelligent, those who are concerned with ideas and ideals, not just with carv-ing out for themselves an easy, remunerative, and possibly shady career.

Party politics as practiced on the campus consume the student's thought and interest when he should be listening to the lecturer or thinking about his studies. Too often they take him out of the lecture room when he should be there. Over and over again one finds an astonishingly high percent-age of examination failures which are due, not to lack of ability, but to inordinate preoccupation with party political activity. Practically any professor who is concerned with ed-ucational values sees party politics as the curse of Latin American university life.

This holds good for most of the universities of Vene-zuela. Understandably, the Communists have exploited the situation. But the hold which the Left has on so many campuses today cannot just be represented as one big Communist plot. There are a great many other people who must share responsibility for the existing situation in which the security authorities regard Venezuela Central University, the "university city" of Caracas, for example, as one big hotbed of intrigue and subversion. In exasperation a man with a considerable responsibility for the security of the country recently told me: "Some day we are just going to reach the end of our tether and bomb the whole damn place."

There is an element of human tragedy in the way in which the present generation of students get so caught up in politics. Once, it was the sons of the "200 families" who were most likely to be found on the campus. Coming from the wealthy ruling group, probably they would in any case in due course spend their lives passing power from one to another, forever engaged in the political intrigue and skulduggery which passed for party politics.

Today many of those attending university come from families who can ill afford to support them there. Other people sacrifice so that they may be given a better chance in life. The new middle class wishes to see its sons and daughters equipped with university education before going into business or the professions. Yet they see their youngsters caught up in the same old pointless activities, with their studies suffering calamitously as a consequence.

The nature of the problem, and the reaction of more serious-minded parents to it, can best be illustrated by citing the story of Caracas' Catholic university. In 1953, during the dictatorship of the corrupt and brutal Pérez Jiménez, the State university in Caracas had been on strike for the whole of one semester. Then some of the students' parents got together and discussed the possibility of starting a university which, being new, could consciously break with the evil and destructive political tradition which was undermining the country's academic life. They went to the bishops, who in turn gave the Jesuits responsibility for the creation of a new university. The Jesuits were already running high schools and, with a couple of hundred of their men already involved in educational work, there was no question of their being able to staff it exclusively with priests, even had they desired to do so. From the start, Venezuela's Catholic university has had a greater proportion of laymen on its top staff than is normally found in such an institution run by a religious order. For example, the vice-president and the deans of most of the various faculties are laymen.

For years, succeeding dictators intervened as of right in the life of every university. As a consequence, when the country at last tried to make an end of dictators and all their works, the various universities were given an exceptional degree of autonomy. The students' associations were permitted to share responsibility for the administration and even the academic life of the universities at every level. Thus student representatives attend, and participate in, all the meetings of the different faculties, even of the board of rectors, where they are fully empowered to vote—a right which they exercise with enthusiasm. But this reverses the normal student-teacher relationship. The student is, as it were, on the board of management. As he sits in the lecture room he is in effect one of the employers of the lecturer from whom he must learn.

In the State universities, directors, deans, and even the rector are elected, after noisy campaigns, by the student body. *Acción Democraticá* still gets the largest number of votes in most universities, although—and this is a sign of the times—the student association with the largest number of members in the country was by 1965 the Christian one. But in four or five of the country's universities the student associations, who are able to play the dominant role in these elections, are controlled by extreme Left-wing groups. It is not surprising in the circumstances that one finds a disproportionate number of Left-wing professors and others on their staffs.

Against this background, Catholic University has stood outside the existing tradition of campus politics. It has as a consequence built itself up as the most serious-minded of any. It is often said that it is the only university in Venezuela where one can be sure of having classes every day, for student strikes and agitations remain a normal feature of the life of other universities.

The Jesuits, who still have responsibility for Catholic University, do not permit political organization on the campus, although politics are discussed in the classroom. With political activity banned, and no campus strikes, it has succeeded in a relatively short time in achieving high academic standards and, in most of its departments, consistently gets the best examination results. Its success is a constant reminder of just how detrimental to their true purpose is the non-stop political activity in the other universities.

CHURCH PROBLEMS

From the political point of view, Dr. Caldera has good reason to be glad that the Venezuelan bishops have not come out and claimed his party as their own. This would help no one. Nevertheless, there must be times when he looks wistfully at the dynamic lead for social change which comes, for example, from the bishops of Chile.

With one or two exceptions Venezuela's bishops have not emerged either at the Vatican Council or at home as being notably on the side of immediate and drastic change. Nevertheless, Venezuela has one bishop, in particular, of a new type now found in most Latin American countries. These are sometimes referred to as the "wooden cross" bishops because some of the best known have dispensed with costly pectoral crosses and, as a gesture of their desire to identify themselves with the poor, have replaced these with simple wooden crosses. Along with the gesture normally goes a life outstanding for its simplicity and its freedom from anything more than the required minimum of ceremonial.

Bishop Feliciano Gonzales of Maracay comes from a working-class background. His father was a cobbler; his brother is a labor leader who is closely associated with Dr. Caldera. Priests working in his diocese proudly told me that Bishop Gonzales "has a real grasp of the revolution which is needed here and which is already beginning to take place."

He is a man of enormous charity who never spares himself. When the latest supply of relief goods arrives from the Caritas organization, he will work for two or three days and nights without stopping, exhausting others who try to keep up with him and causing anxiety to those who hope that such a man may be with them for a long time on this earth.

His home is open to his people; his mind, open to new ideas. He is at the center of endless discussions which always concern the search for answers to the problems of his people. Remedial charity is not enough today. He is concerned with preventive charity—finding positive answers to age-old social problems, initiating schemes which may provide a cure, not first-aid treatment alone, for present ills.

The Church's contribution to the development of Venezuela is seriously limited by the number of priests available, and this in turn is limited by the number of vocations to the priesthood. These tend to be few and far between. It is interesting that there are many Catholics outside Latin America who talk of Mexico as though it were practically under Communist rule and of Venezuela as a very Catholic country. Yet one is far more likely to find packed churches in Mexico than in Venezuela. And, side by side with this, goes the fact that reportedly one-third of the seminarians of Latin America are in Mexico, which now sends priests to other countries of the sub-continent.

Venezuela has been "Catholic" for over 400 years, but it is said to have the lowest vocation rate in the whole of Latin America. In Caracas between 1957 and 1964 only eight priests were ordained to work in this diocese of over one million Catholics. During the same period, according to Philip J. Cunningham, C.S.P., the population of the area increased by 200,000. Only one quarter of the priests in Venezuela today are native-born.

In the United States of America there is one priest for every 770 Catholics; in Venezuela, one for every 5,000. At the parish level there is one for every 10,000. Directly related to this is the fact that only 25 per cent of Venezuelans are married according to the Church; some 15 per cent go to Mass on Sunday (and this means that 85 per cent do not); and a mere 12 per cent of the country's children have six or more years' education.

Behind the shortage of local-born priests lies a long story, not always a pretty one, but one that is all too common in Latin America. For many years there was a constant and bitter struggle between the Spanish-born priests, known as the "Spaniards," and the "colonial-born," or "Creoles," born in Venezuela which was at that time Spain's colony.

During the long struggle for independence there were periods when "Spanish" bishops would not ordain "Creoles" to the priesthood. Then came independence and a swing in the opposite direction. The constitution ordered that all bishops in Venezuela must be native-born. Thus vocations to the priesthood became a political shuttlecock.

These problems of the past have their repercussions to this day. For example, the large number of "Spanish" clergy still makes entry into the priesthood unacceptable to many native-born Venezuelans.

There is no great tradition in most Latin American countries of the faithful collectively supporting the Church with their regular offerings. A consequence is that Venezuelan priests must live mainly by the stipends they receive for baptisms, marriages, and funerals. As one priest put it, "to the poor the priest appears as the harsh extortioner of what little money they have and to the rich as little better than a beggar."

The attitude of the Latin American male in general and of the Venezuelan male in particular toward his "manliness" is yet another factor which seriously militates against the flow of vocations to the priesthood. In an article entitled "Machismo and the priestly vocation" (*Catholic World*, June, 1964), Father Andrew Weigert, S.J., stated that in the Latin Americans' idea of manliness (*machismo*) there is a strong emphasis on sexual prowess. The *macho completo*, or complete man, must be able to dominate women, and the evidence of his sexual potency is provided by the number of children he can father—in or out of any regular union.

The priest on the other hand is an *hombre de faldas*, a man in skirts, celibate, and concerned with religion, which is a woman's matter. The choice is therefore too often seen as between being a man and being a priest. It is not surprising that a survey showed that only six per cent of Catholic parents would welcome one of their sons becoming a priest.

The Edmonite Fathers, the first U.S. missionary group to come to Caracas, had been established there for only a matter of months when I stayed with them in 1965. By then the forceful and progressive Maryknoll Fathers were already planning to move some of their men into Venezuela in a much bigger way. It is likely that many more North American priests will go there in the next few years.

It remains to be seen whether, as the process develops, the Communists and anti-clericals will succeed in working up a campaign against the "Yankee clerical invasion."

The increasing numbers of priests now going from Spain to most parts of Latin America in response to Rome's call will obviously lead to a significant contribution being made to Venezuela's chronic shortage of clergy. Again, it has still to be seen what reception they will get, as their numbers mount, from those who in the past distinguished so clearly between "Spanish" and "native-born" clergy. But as the flow of priests arriving from other European countries builds up, it is reasonable to suppose that the Spanish versus Venezuelan problem will diminish in importance.

ENLIGHTENED SELF-INTEREST

I first heard of Venezuela's "voluntary dividend" scheme from the Papal Nuncio who quoted it as one of the country's most encouraging developments, not directly Christian in its organization and inspiration, but truly Christian in its intent. The scheme is a practical recognition by sections of big and not-so-big business that they have a genuine interest in the country's development and the well-being of its people as a whole.

Enlightened self-interest has become something of a cant phrase, yet it can have very real meaning. The activities of the cement industry on behalf of rural people brought this home to me when I was in Venezuela in 1961. A section of the industry, I found, was making it its business to take, by means of films, lectures, and practical advice, education in rural development and personal hygiene to some of the most backward parts of the country.

Hookworm is passed around most frequently by an absence of any sort of sanitation. Its victims, who are numbered in millions all over the developing areas of the world, suffer from chronic inertia. What often looks like an unwillingness to do anything on their own behalf is thus quite frequently not unwillingness, but physical inability. To teach such people the rudiments of personal hygiene and sanitation, then to encourage them to build themselves the first lavatory they have ever had, along with its own little cesspool, is clearly a sensible and humane thing to do. Equally, to encourage them to keep their pigs in clean and properly designed sties as opposed to leaving them to scavenge (and, if the unpleasant truth be bold, to be the household's sanitary system) is good sense and good socio-economics. In both cases it is also good for the cement industry, since latrines and pig sties alike are built with cement.

This may be an obvious way for big business to think, but it is not the way it has always thought. Too often in the past the developing area was seen as one into which a monopoly could move with the idea of getting quick profits regardless of the interests of the people concerned, and often in direct conflict with them.

In Latin America today both types of foreign operators may be found, but one noteworthy sign of change is that the number of the first, who see it as being in their own interests to help the country, as opposed to the second, who are only concerned to "mine" it of its natural wealth, is growing.

The voluntary dividend scheme to which the Nuncio drew my attention is just about as enlightened as one is likely to find anywhere. And it is not, incidentally, confined to big monopolies.

The dividend organization is based on a self-imposed tax. The giants among its members are Creole Oil, an American concern, and Shell Oil, but altogether some 330 firms are involved, including about half of the larger Venezuelan enterprises. Each allocates from two to five per cent of its profits to the scheme, five per cent being the maximum the law allows anyone to deduct for income tax purposes. The percentage varies because no one is then able to deduce from the sum allocated what are any particular firm's profits in any one year.

Much of the drive comes from Creole which was already, before the scheme began, doing much good work for the development of the country. The aim of the voluntary dividend organization is to co-ordinate, guide, and make overall plans for the various social development projects undertaken by its members and so to accelerate the progress and development of the entire country. Those involved are far-sighted enough to be able to recognize that rapid development, spread as evenly as possible throughout the economy, is very much in their own interest as well as in that of the country as a whole.

Development of a type which includes the largest possible number of people and the widest possible groups means a steadily increasing consumer public. The tendency in Venezuela, as in so many other countries which have a single profitable raw material to sell on the world's markets, is for development to be uneven, with one section of the public benefiting while the rest are left largely untouched. This until recently has been the situation in Venezuela whose oil has brought considerable wealth to a few and has led to development racing ahead in one or two cities while the vast mass of the people continue to live in ignorance and poverty.

There are some 300,000 unemployed to 2,500,000 employed workers; another 80,000 youngsters come on to the labor market each year.

One of the dividend scheme's most successful activities has been the providing of pre-vocational training. The people of a particular *barrio* (village) are persuaded to build their own school. Either the scheme as a whole or one of its members, such as Creole, provides the materials and equipment. It also provides one metal, one woodwork, and one drawing teacher. The Ministry of Education pays the salaries once the school is established. In a score or more of these self-help schools, boys of ten to fifteen years of age now receive an education which will prepare them for more advanced technical training so that they may ultimately go on to become craftsmen in their own villages. Creole executives, who have sponsored this particular scheme, told me that they hope in the next phase of the program to establish another three dozen such schools with some 200 boys to the school.

Members of the dividend scheme have between them opened more than 120 secondary schools in urban slums where only six years of primary school education had previously been available.

In 1958, when Creole was still thinking in terms of pilot schemes, they entered into an agreement with the government to establish a college for the training of rural teachers. In order to get it launched, teachers from the United States were brought in. Some 240,000 U.S. dollars were put into it by this one oil company. In due course, once it had proved its success, AID took up the scheme. In 1964 a second teacher training school was established. The teachers from these colleges are trained in the needs of the rural population, with particular emphasis on agriculture for the boys and sewing and home economics for the girls. These two projects will ensure an ever-growing stream of qualified rural teachers whose aim will be to bring new life to the villages.

Normally there is a tendency for the products of teacher training colleges to make for the cities as soon as their training is completed. But the sort of training given in these

Creole-sponsored schools ensures that they will stay where they are most needed.

One interesting aspect of the scheme is that this big oil monopoly consciously aims to produce what it describes as "micro-industrialists"—people at the very opposite end of the industrial scale to Creole itself. These are young men trained to be village craftsmen, metal workers, woodworkers, furniture makers, smiths, and so on. Too frequently, Creole argues, technical schools in developing countries provide training identical to that given in similar institutions in fully developed countries, with the predictable result that there are increasing numbers of people with skills that are not required and who therefore are unemployed, bitter, and frustrated. "Our schools," Creole executives told me, "will not produce people who will be knocking at the doors of big firms for jobs that are not there. But they will be equipped to meet the needs of their local communities."

The dividend scheme is increasingly making the smaller, local industrialists, too, think in terms of overall economic and social growth, not just of the narrow interests of their own enterprises. Underlying the whole thing is the belief that the next 25 years are going to be the ones of greatest change and therefore the greatest tension. "If we fail in this period," say its sponsors, "then we are lost."

The motivation behind the dividend scheme is obviously a mixed one. It does not require much imagination to see that foreign monopolies operating in developing countries are vulnerable. A hostile or Left-wing government nowadays does not hesitate to expropriate the assets of the big oil concern functioning within its borders. If this were to happen to Creole, it would lose everything, for it operates only in Venezuela. For the local industrialists who have come into the scheme, steady, peaceful development spread as widely as possible over the population would clearly be in their interests. Conversely, a period of political turbulence and, still more, a Communist take-over would end all their hopes of continuing expansion.

Fear of Communism obviously plays its part in encouraging support for the scheme. One man concerned with its organization put it quite crudely to me: "There will be 600,000,000 Latin Americans by the time the United States has a population of 300,000,000," he said. "Whether they are going to do as China's 600,000,000 did depends on what we do now."

But in the case of some of the moving spirits behind the scheme, there is genuine Christian motivation too.

The idea of the voluntary dividend scheme is being copied in some Latin American countries, Peru and Chile among them, and studied in others. It is one that is likely to spread.

THE COMMUNISTS' TWO LINES

Anyone who wishes to have an indication of the way in which Communists may be expected to behave under conditions in which a resort to arms is a present possibility, no matter whether it be in Asia, Africa, or Latin America, should study the activities of Venezuela's Communists.

Until recently, Moscow and Peking both took the view that in Venezuela the armed struggle could be combined with the constitutional struggle. And as in the case of Guatemala, Moscow tended to put the greater emphasis on constitutional struggle, Peking on the armed struggle.

At that time any Communist party in a developing

country where the terrain was suitable and arms were available could be sure of the blessing of both Communist capitals if it tried to raise guerilla bands and at the same time use democracy for Communist ends.

This is what the pro-Moscow Venezuelan Communist party attempted to do. In accord with Moscow's line it aimed to continue to use legal trade unions, peasant unions, and sympathetic political organizations, even while some of its members were busy establishing insurrectionary centers.

This line, it was thought, provided the opportunity to slowly build up a guerilla force and yet at the same time to continue to drain the last bit of benefit to be had from democracy right up to the moment when the guerilla armies would sweep from the mountains and jungles into the capital city for the final seizure of power. It all sounded splendid in Communist ears, but it did not work out that way.

In 1961 the Communist party of Venezuela, whose leaders are rated high in world Communist circles, started preparations for illegal activity. In 1962 it went over to armed struggle. At approximately the same time MIR (Revolutionary Movement of the Left), a mixed group of Marxist revolutionaries with a generally Castro-Peking-orientated approach to the question of revolution, went over to violence too. By 1965 the PCV (Communist Party of Venezuela) had some 1,200 guerillas in the field and MIR approximately 300. The PCV was the dominant group in the West, while MIR was the more powerful in the East. These figures are exclusive of an unknown number of urban terrorists who provided town bases for both guerilla forces and who maintained a campaign of audacious raids, kidnappings, and killings.

In addition to the total of some 1,500 trained guerillas loosely united within F.A.L.N. (Armed Forces of National Liberation), the Communists, it was estimated in 1965, had perhaps ten times that number who actively supported them and might join them if the call were made. Shortly after this the government launched a military campaign against some of the guerilla strongholds. The guerillas suffered serious losses. The guerilla problem, it was said, was this time finally settled. Then, in November, 1966, began a new round of guerilla activities and urban terrorism. A number of policemen were murdered, and an attempt was made on the life of the army's Commander-in-Chief. In March, 1967, Dr. Iribarren Borges, brother of Venezuela's Foreign Minister, was murdered by terrorists.

The PCV had its guerilla units in the western states of Falcon and Lara. Here, many of the guerillas belong to the areas in which they operate. The rural family group in Venezuela is so extensive that, in some areas at least, there is hardly a family without some member a guerilla. And family ties are so strong that no member of a family can be expected to denounce another. This obviously creates serious problems for security authorities charged with the job of putting down their activities.

Time after time, the government announces, as it did in December, 1964, and again in 1966, that the army has virtually wiped out the guerillas of a given area. Then, as likely as not, a couple of days later the guerillas seize the town which is the heart of that area. This is an act of defiance against the government, and it is also intended to drive the point firmly into the minds of the local populace that it is the Communist guerillas, not the government, who have the last word.

Among the insurgents have been at times military and naval defectors. A number of marines joined the guerillas after one particular mutiny. The evidence suggests that a good percentage of the guerillas were actual members either of the PCV or of the splinter groups attached to MIR. MIR provided most of the terrorists. In practice, the Communist party during 1966 split as between the hard- and soft-liners. Peking and Havana wooed both groups, and have had a fair degree of success.

Following the normal Moscow line for such areas, PCV worked to try to have a broad, united revolutionary front. F.A.L.N. provided some sort of basis for an uneasy alliance of what may be called "the fighting Left," but tensions between Castroites, Moscowites, Pekingites, and others were considerable.

Then in 1967 came Moscow's shock decision. As part of its peaceful co-existence policy it began to urge that where constitutional struggle was possible there should be no armed struggle. The pro-Moscow PCV decided to abandon armed struggle, which meant abandoning its allies in the field.

Most of those guerillas who have been captured or killed have been under the age of 26, many of them only 18 to 20 years of age. When the armed struggle first began, the small guerilla bands were largely made up of urban members—workers and particularly students who took to the hills. Perhaps more dangerous for the future is the growth of groups mainly composed of local campesinos.

The insurgents' acts of terrorism in Caracas and other cities have gained worldwide publicity because of their planning, audacity, and ferocity. Again, the aim would appear to be to demonstrate that they can strike when, where, and whom they please. One favorite means of achieving this is to pick up an intelligence officer or member of the U.S. military mission, see that the kidnapping is widely publicized, hold him for some days, then release him blindfolded, stark naked, and in broad daylight in the heart of the city—to the merriment, or dismay, of the public according to its political sympathies. Another is to announce that a policeman will be killed on the streets of the capital city each day for a given period of time and then remorselessly to carry this into effect.

It is easy to suppose, as Moscow so clearly did, that by running the constitutional and armed struggles simultaneously, Communists can get the best of both worlds. The experience of the Moscow-line Communists of Venezuela, however, suggests that the opposite may be the case. The party's association with guerilla activities in the rural areas and with terrorism in the towns alienated solid industrial workers and trade unionists who once gave it their support and upon whom the party, according to its own Marxist-Leninist teaching, must ultimately rely. Even though Moscow's foreign policy interests influenced the decision to pull out, it seems clear that the party suffered rather than gained by the attempt to run two lines at once.

However, the various Communist organizations, despite their differences and difficulties, still continue to attract impatient, idealistic youngsters to their cause and, in particular, to the armed struggle. It has been from the universities that some of the most dedicated young revolutionaries have come. One priest who had been into the mountains to hear the confessions of guerillas declared that in a different age most of them would have been crusaders.

In a number of cases it has been students who have been responsible for establishing guerilla bases in remote rural areas. A carefully selected group of revolutionary students within a university will disappear. They will probably include a young doctor or medical student, a nurse, a couple of young agronomists, and perhaps one or two girls who are domestic science students. In due course they will turn up in some place in the mountains which is well suited to guerilla warfare. But they do not at once engage in guerilla activities.

The doctor and nurse bring healing to an area where no medical help has ever before been taken. The agronomists will teach the local people how to improve their soil, their crops, their methods of husbandry. The domestic science students will move among the women teaching them how to extract the last gram of nutritional value from the food they prepare, how to make their homes better places for their men to live in, how to take better care of their children.

The infantile mortality rate goes down. Life gets better for the people. With good reason they see the little group of dedicated town dwellers, who have sacrificed all to live among them, as the best friends they ever had. Neither the Church, the Government, nor, still less, the Army ever did anything like this for poor people such as they. Before long they will gladly risk their lives to protect these new and proven friends.

It is at this stage, when a "popular base" has been well established, that the arms begin to come in. The little group is joined by other, more experienced Communists, and together they practice the art of guerilla warfare. One more "foco" or revolutionary center, with its roots among the people, has been established.

As likely as not, members of the group have already received some training in the use of small arms, hand grenades, and similar weapons while they were at the university. Time after time the police raid the hospitals and university buildings within the university city which, Spanish style, is a city within a city. Almost, one might say, it is a turbulent, autonomous republic within the capital city itself. The police leave with trucks piled high with submachine guns, tommy guns, a wide variety of weapons, and an immense amount of ammunition. Their biggest haul on one occasion was taken from a hostel run for girl students by an order of nuns best known for its educational work on behalf of the daughters of the very rich.

There is a more or less constant two-way movement of students between the universities and the guerilla areas. Students take to the mountains, spend some time drilling and establishing bases, then come back to resume their studies or, as frequently happens, because their health has broken down.

Since students, if they are going to be Left at all, will generally be as Left as they can, it is MIR, the ultra-Leftist and most politically irresponsible group, which tends to gain their allegiance, and not the more disciplined and "moderate" PCV.

All over the developing areas today, Communists talk of "a long and arduous struggle" when they take to arms. It remains to be seen whether those of Venezuela, who are trying to build up a "people's army" from their scattered guerilla bases, will be able to hold their own against the attacks of security forces in the mountains, and at the same time continue to hold their supporters among the workers and students in the towns. The logic of the situation is leading to the strengthening of the pro-Peking and Castro groups at the expense of the Moscow-line Communist party. When the first meeting of the Organisation for Latin American Solidarity (OLAS) was held in Havana in August 1967, members of a wide variety of Marxist revolutionary bodies were brought together from all over the subcontinent. The PCV was conspicuous by its absence. For the moment, at any rate, Venezuela's revolutionary torch had passed to the representatives of the more aggressive but less experienced and disciplined splinter groups whose inspiration comes from Havana and Peking and whose darling is Che Guevara.

Self-Help and Violence

5

It was Sunday morning, and I was attending Mass at an ancient Franciscan church not far from my hotel in Bogota, Colombia. We had just reached the *Introit*, early in the Mass, when through the open church door came the noise of what appeared to be a powerful motorcycle from which the silencer had been removed. A few minutes later another started up, then another and another.

The noise outside grew in volume. It seemed possible that those responsible were deliberately driving round and round the church with engines roaring. I decided that the only possible explanation was that they were anti-clericals who, in the worst Latin American tradition, were out to destroy the Mass for others.

Not one word of the sermon was audible to anyone in the congregation. The ear-splitting racket continued right to the end of Mass. My indignation had risen with the volume of the sound, and as soon as the last word of the Mass had been said, I shot out through the door to see who was responsible.

It was neither some Latin American equivalent of

"mods and rockers," nor yet anti-clericals. The sons of the
local well-to-do, members of a go-kart club, were using as a
race track the roads encircling a small block of buildings
which included no less than four churches. They were doing
so with the cooperation of the police who had diverted the
traffic to suit their convenience. But whoever timed and
sited the races in this way had clearly no thought for the
convenience of worshipers, no concern for religious suscep-
tibilities.

When one of the Franciscan priests came out into the
street at the end of Mass, it was quite apparent that he did
not view the episode as being in any way exceptional, for he
stood for a while watching the races with as much enjoy-
ment as anyone.

The lack of social responsibility which characterizes
certain sectors of Latin American life is something that
must be appreciated if one is to understand some of the
difficulties which confront those who work for social
change. Concern for the convenience and welfare of others
normally plays some part, at least, in motivating attempts
at social betterment. But numbers of Latin Americans, of
the educated and moneyed classes in particular, seem totally
insensitive to such matters. This is not only apparent in
their treatment of the poor. It literally shouts at you as you
observe their dealings with each other.

The idea which seemed almost, though not quite, uni-
versally to be accepted by the wealthy in mid-Victorian
England, that the poor were somehow responsible for their
own poverty and that this had something to do with sin
still survives in similar circles in Latin America to this day.
Those who work for the social betterment of the poor must
operate against this background. It explains in part why

self-help schemes for those in need find particular favor among the well-to-do, for thereby their own responsibility is reduced to a minimum. This is not to decry the schemes as such, and those concerned with social problems in other areas of the world can undoubtedly learn quite a lot from the self-help schemes of Latin America and of Colombia in particular.

SELF-HELP HOUSING

Dr. Fabio Robledo, a warm and cultured man, is head of Colombia's biggest housing organization, the *Instituto de Crédito Territorial*. He represents a group of Latin American countries on the United Nations' Housing Committee. On his desk in his office in Bogota he keeps a photostatic copy of a 400-year-old plan of the city as a reminder that town planning is not new in Latin America. The old Spanish colonial plan shows the entire area laid out in orderly blocks, with four houses to the block and 50 blocks set around a plaza. But Dr. Fabio Robledo is acutely aware that the Spaniards—with all the country at their disposal—had far fewer problems than he has today.

Around the cities of every Latin American country there are immense slums, the result of the flight from the land. But in many countries the capital city is almost the only one of any size. Colombia has many more cities than most, and each has its own acute housing problem. To add to the difficulties, these cities are scattered around a country which is approximately two and a half times the size of united Germany, with not much more than one-quarter of its population.

The large scale flight from the land is a relatively new

problem; it has become acute only in the last 10 or 15 years. The country's population grows by something like three per cent a year, but the rate of growth in the cities is some seven to eight per cent. Bogota's rate of increase is one of the biggest in the world.

To provide this fast-growing population with any sort of housing fit for human habitation is a very considerable problem. And how to provide the necessary "utilities" is at least as big. Even with a more ready public acceptance of state planning and municipal building, and with more material resources and human skills on which to draw, any European country would still have difficulty in keeping up with a population growth such as this. But Colombia's government has limited resources. Moreover, it has no great love of state planning and believes that the emphasis should be upon self-help rather than state help.

This emphasis upon self-help has led, under Dr. Fabio Robledo's guidance, to an extraordinary proliferation of schemes of one sort or another, some of which may well have lessons for more developed countries whose problems are smaller and whose resources are larger.

The most widely publicized, though not necessarily the most successful, is Kennedy City, the new satellite town built on an old airport within ten minutes' car ride of Bogota's main industrial sector.

Kennedy City is entirely residential. Most of its 15,000 houses, with their 100,000 inhabitants, have been built on a self-help, home-ownership basis. No fewer than 6,000 were built in their spare time by the families who live in them. It is claimed to be the largest self-help housing project in the world, made possible by financial aid which came through the American Alliance for Progress. The first brick of the first house was laid by the late President John F. Kennedy.

Most of the people who live there came from the slums, and it may be said that their present housing conditions are better than what they knew in the past. But there is, of course, a tendency for houses built by amateurs to be of lower quality than those built by professionals. And while house-ownership is an admirable aim, an element of disillusionment may quickly enter into the people's thinking when payment for what is manifestly a substandard house has to be extended over a period of, say, 20 years.

The critics of Kennedy City point to the large numbers of little houses with just two rooms; even the cooking must be done outside. In the tropical lowlands of Colombia this might be endurable, but Bogota happens to be situated some 8,000 feet up in the Andes, making it one of the highest capital cities in the world and among the coolest in Latin America. To the families who moved in from ramshackle shanties with no modern facilities, building a little two-roomed house of this sort may well be exciting at the time. But what, people ask, will they be like in 20 years? May it not be that for a large part of the period in which the mortgage is being paid the property will be practically worthless?

Another criticism is that a minimum of land has been allocated to each house, which leaves no room for expansion. In other words, there is no opportunity for the man with the growing family to add to the size of his tiny dwelling even if he would. This is, however, but one of Colombia's many self-help housing schemes.

"As planners, we have the greatest fecundity in the whole world," Dr. Fabio Robledo told me. His organization promotes, in all, a dozen different types of self-help projects.

One of I.C.T.'s ways of encouraging self-help is to build just the outer shell of a house. The family who lives in it then completes it, putting in window frames, doors, and all the interior fittings. They buy the plot of land, the shell, and all the materials for the house on easy payments which stretch over some 20 years.

Another of I.C.T.'s schemes is to sell on installments a plot of land to a would-be house-owner. When the plot has been purchased, I.C.T. advances another loan so that he may build a house on the site.

Yet another, specifically aimed at stimulating private enterprise, is called the "Three Parties Plan." I.C.T. advances one-third of the cost; the future owner puts down another one-third; and the remainder is advanced by an insurance company.

There is a plan to encourage employers to house their workers. This is a joint venture by means of which the government provides financial assistance to the employer from whom the worker rents his house. The rents which are paid normally add up to 30 to 50 per cent of the worker's salary —a very substantial percentage indeed.

These and other self-help schemes are being experimented with in some 20 different cities. Dr. Fabio Robledo claims that it is the biggest self-help experiment in the world. He argues that Colombia's rural people, like most of those of Latin America, normally build their houses, which they therefore own. These may be, and almost invariably are, small, rough-and-ready, inadequate. Yet, even so, the people who come from the rural areas to the cities already have a tradition of building and owning their little substandard homes. It has still to be shown whether a tradition which grew out of the conditions obtaining in remote rural areas can be thus transplanted and adapted to the needs of great modern cities.

There can be no doubt about the size and urgency of the problem with which I.C.T. is trying to deal. Dr. Fabio Robledo reduced it to simple arithmetic for me. By law, since I.C.T. must select the largest families as candidates for its projects, the average works out at nine people to each of its houses; and in the majority of cases families grow at the rate of a baby a year.

There is at present a shortage of 300,000 urban houses. Existing government and private building programs combined produce only 40,000 per annum. An absolute minimum of 60,000 is required if the present admittedly inadequate housing standards are to be maintained. An optimum plan of 90,000 would eliminate the shortage. But no one has dared yet to think in terms of such a figure.

The planners are held back, not only by a shortage of money, but, what is perhaps more difficult to meet, an inability to produce the necessary bricks, tiles, cement, and other building materials. For the national housing plan to be stepped up to existing needs, a whole range of industries would have to be extended far beyond anything which is made possible by the country's present supply of skilled personnel.

In these circumstances, Dr. Fabio Robledo argues, it is necessary to choose between quantity and quality; there can, on the basis of the type of projects which the government now approves, be no question of building for quality. Quantity is the decisive factor. The U.S.S.R., he says, had to make the same choice after the Revolution, and it, too, chose quantity rather than quality. Russia had no alternative, and neither has Colombia.

Visitors may well be justifiably impressed by the ingenuity and enthusiasm of those who must try every solution other than the state solution. But they may also be left pondering the thought that, just as there can be doctrinaire socialists, so also there can be doctrinaire supporters of free enterprise.

In the minds of Colombia's ruling class and many of its political and ecclesiastical leaders any form of state intervention smacks of socialism. There is usually little attempt to distinguish between this and Communism. Moreover, they are often confirmed in their attitudes by representatives of U.S. agencies which provide financial assistance to approved projects and who see the establishment of a free enterprise society, which has grown out of North America's history, as being ideally suited, also, to Latin America.

SELF-HELP STUDENTS

In the field of higher education, Colombia puts her main emphasis on do-it-yourself studies. And, as in the case of housing, the government throws its weight behind non-government organizations.

Instituto Colombiano de Especialización Técnica en el Exterior (ICETEX) is the agency which has the overall responsibility for providing financial assistance to the country's students. This is always on the basis of loans, not state subsidies.

ICETEX was started twelve years ago by Señor M. Betancourt, who is now an Assistant-Director of UNESCO. In his youth he won a scholarship while working in a factory. He asked his employers for a loan to go overseas for his studies; they agreed on condition that he repay it in due course. ICETEX grew out of that experience.

Begun with 40,000 dollars, it has by now, Gerardo Eusse Hoyes, its present director, explained to me, "invested seven million dollars in the youth of this country." Its main work is to provide loans for students to enable them to graduate and for graduates who wish to go abroad to get what Colombia cannot offer. The program was from the start made possible by private companies who were persuaded to back it financially. This has continued to be the main basis of the organization's work; seventy per cent of its funds now come in this way.

In the 15 years from 1950 to 1965 the number of university students in the whole country multiplied five times over, from 8,000 to 40,000. If the present program is successful, this number will be doubled by 1970. Since the majority of students cannot afford to pay their own way, ICETEX must constantly be persuading its backers to put more and more money into its projects. Since the money is loaned to the students, it is loans, not gifts, which ICETEX seeks.

It sees its rôle as that of a trustee. On the basis of a very careful selection system, ICETEX guarantees the quality of a student, advances him a loan on which two per cent interest is paid, then recovers it over a period which is normally twice that of the studies. Repayment begins one year after the completion of studies. That there are very few defaulters is an indication of the good selection system which has been developed, but ICETEX is also assisted by legislation which empowers an employer to deduct the promised amount from the defaulter's wages. In practice this has only been invoked three times in the organization's history. If a graduate has difficulty in finding a job, ICE-TEX, which is kept informed by employers of their special needs, helps to find him appropriate work.

Since 80 per cent of the country's students are now assisted by it, ICETEX clearly has a very considerable say in the selection and enrollment of students and also in their subsequent employment.

It is currently trying to persuade students to go into fields which will qualify them to make the greatest possible contribution to the development of their country. Its first priority is education; second comes public and private administration. In 1958 only 1.7 per cent of the country's students were training for the teaching profession; by 1965 this had risen to eight per cent, but this, too, falls very short of the nation's urgent needs. The students' own priorities are in almost inverse ratio to those of ICETEX. First in the students' choice comes engineering, then social sciences, law, medicine, agriculture, in that order. Education along with agriculture ranks a very bad fifth.

Nothing has so far been found to divert the young Colombian's enthusiasm for engineering, for which by far the largest number opt despite the fact that the openings are still very limited. Every engineering school in the country has come into existence in the last fifteen years. When they first opened, it was believed that there would be a great need for engineers, but there is a danger that before long far more engineering graduates will be pouring out from the universities than industry can hope to absorb. The engineering schools' enrollment has doubled in the last four years, with no corresponding growth in capacity on the part of industry to make use of their services. If the present trend is maintained, a great deal of frustration lies ahead.

ICETEX has learned from experience a lesson which is applicable to most countries in a hurry to develop: the natural thing is to suppose that the first step on the way to development is to produce engineers and civil engineers. But before these industries can get the skilled and semi-skilled labor they require if they are to develop, a crash program in popular education is needed. For this the country must have teachers. Yet the teaching profession is usually so poorly-paid that it is among the least attractive of any.

Here, it seems to me, both the strength and weakness of this work of ICETEX is revealed. It is in a unique position to discover what are genuine priorities. And it has an interest in steering students into work which will enable them to repay the loans it has advanced. The individual student knows that for years after graduating he will have to make regular repayments on the loan which was granted him as a young would-be student. The tendency will, therefore, be for the student to select a field of studies where the course is as short as possible and which will lead on to work which brings quick and high remuneration. This must surely help to explain, for example, why so relatively few choose medicine, which is one of the country's greatest needs. The man who spends six years at his medical studies will, in due course, as a young and not particularly well paid doctor, have for another 12 years a financial millstone around his neck. The position of the poorly-paid teacher or agriculturalist may be even worse. The engineering student should be able in a relatively short period to get through his studies with the hope of a remunerative job in industry which will enable him quickly and easily to repay the loan.

For the student going abroad, ICETEX's services are absolutely essential. It keeps in touch with universities all over the world, advises which is most appropriate for the man or woman who wishes to do post-graduate studies and in addition—and this can be decisive—arranges the necessary currency exchange.

Some Colombians argue that this system of personal loans, like that of self-help home building, makes for sturdy independence and a growth of individualism. Its critics say that to the normal worries and frustrations of the student, and of the young graduate trying to make his way in life, are added financial anxieties and the handicap of beginning one's working life deeply in debt.

In its favor, it may be said that there is a very definite limit to the amount of direct financial aid which the government of a developing country can afford to give. Without some such loan scheme a high proportion of Colombia's students might never have the opportunity to go to university at all. A number of other Latin American countries, including Panama, Peru, and Venezuela, have recently become interested in the formation of a similar organization because they believe that only something like this can help them, despite their limited resources, to quickly produce the graduates they require.

SELF-HELP RADIO

In 1947, Monsignor José Joaquín Salcedo, a priest in Sutatenza, a mountain town 80 miles from Bogota, started a radio station by means of which he hoped to be able to educate adult illiterates in his scattered parish. Before long "radio schools" were springing up throughout the area, with

Radio Sutatenza as their center. This was the first attempt at mass adult education by radio in Latin America. It has become perhaps the largest scheme of its type in the world. Operated by an organization called *Acción Cultural Popular*, with Monsignor Salcedo as its head, it is today a three million dollar enterprise receiving aid from the Church, the government, and private foundations.

Its aim from the start was to bring literacy to the people of the rural areas. But it also aimed at something more. While the *campesinos* were learning their alphabet from its radio education programs, they would at the same time be taught their faith, the Church's social teachings, personal hygiene, health, soil improvement, and good husbandry. Together these would help to lift them out of degrading poverty into the dignity which was their right as human beings.

Similar schemes, inspired by *Radio Sutatenza*, have sprung up in ten Latin American countries. Often those responsible for them have been foreign priests who have set up small local transmitters and a few radio schools in their parishes. The Maryknoll Fathers' radio schools in Bolivia are among some of the best known and most successful of these. Monsignor Salcedo's scheme also inspired Brazil's *Movimento de Educação de Base* (MEB) which has carried his ideas still further and developed them in new and interesting ways.

By means of the radio schools, hundreds of thousands of people have by now been given some degree of literacy and have learned something of their religion. And these are in areas where there was practically no hope of schools being built in the foreseeable future nor of priests being available to instruct the people in their faith.

I first became aware of the work of *Radio Sutatenza* when I was in Latin America in 1954. It was then relatively little known, but it seemed to me to be one of the most exciting and promising developments. There was still much of the pioneering spirit about it at that time. Lay leaders were being taught to go into the villages and, with the help of a small radio, blackboard, and textbooks, open up the possibility of a new life for the people. It was a real missionary job.

Today, the project has its critics, although the mere fact of their existence is an indication that Latin America is moving forward in its thinking. The scheme, they say, is directed only towards the rural areas, yet hundreds of thousands of rural people come to live in the towns, and illiteracy is, therefore, now to be found on a vast scale in the urban areas too. Again, the critics say that to make rural people literate is not enough. Unless "alphabetization" goes hand in hand with agrarian reform, it leads only to frustration. Learning to read and write must lead on to the creation of organizations which will enable people to work for their own social uplift. This means creating producers' co-operatives, credit unions, and other organizations.

But unless these, too, are not to be frustrated, road building, irrigation schemes, and similar projects will be needed in order that the area concerned may begin to develop. MEB, in Brazil, has tried to translate these ideas into action. In this sense, it has left the original scheme behind. But even if Monsignor Salcedo's original project had done no more than start so much, it would have splendidly justified its existence.

THE VIOLENCE

The murder of a prominent Liberal politician, Jorge Eliécer Gaitán, in April, 1948, led to a rising in Bogota against the Conservatives. The rising was accompanied by quite exceptional violence and brutality. I remember one Colombian telling me shortly afterward that he had himself seen men worming their way through the hysterical crowds, slashing double-bladed knives to right and left, chopping feet from living bodies.

The story seemed to me at the time to be incredible. But Colombia's subsequent history makes it mild by comparison with some of the things that have since been done. For ten years, all over the country, supporters of the Liberals and Conservatives fought each other. The poorer the area, the more restless the people, the more likely was there to be a blood-letting. Support for one party or another had little to do with political understanding, still less with ideology. Most often it sprang from allegiance to a particular corrupt local political leader.

Appalled and shamed by what had happened, the Conservative and Liberal leaders patched up their differences at the national level and came to an agreement that they should for a specified period in turn provide the country's presidents. But too many people had been killed, too many families bereaved, too many had been caught up in senseless feuds for this to stop the slaughter in the remote areas. The violence dragged on over the years until many of those involved in the non-stop killing had little idea of how it had all begun. By now, most frequently, they are in any case the sons of those who started it all.

What had begun as an allegedly political, undeclared civil war degenerated in time to banditry or, where sadism seems completely to have taken over, brutality for brutality's sake. Killing became the only trade many of those involved had ever known. Estimates vary as to the number who have died since 1948 in "the violence"—as it is called —but it is rarely put at less than one-third of a million. The story is a frightening reminder of how whole communities of people may be degraded when their living conditions are already degrading.

It is estimated that 60 per cent of the land of Colombia is in the hands of four per cent of the people. Only a very small percentage of this is cultivated. Yet there are other regions, where the soil is poorest, usually in the mountains, into which the rural poor are crowded. Quite frequently they live in areas which, having no contact or means of communication of any sort with the outside world, are ones where time has stood still. To social misery have been added almost unbelievably cruel family feuds and banditry which is accompanied by sheer savagery.

There is no doubt that the Communists, although not directly responsible for the original assassination which triggered the civil war, exploited it to the full, even though it required little prompting from them. But as the fighting degenerated into feuding and banditry, with the sons of the fathers who had been killed proceeding to kill each other over the years, the Communists stood aside from the whole thing.

A Marxist commentator, Régis Debray, has described it as a "vast cataclysm which reached depths of cruelty unexperienced in any other war." In *New Left Review*, No. 33, he wrote:

"With the exception of the areas of Galilea, El Pato, Sumapaz, and the guerilla front south of Tolima, where the

Communist party succeeded in establishing a unified command of the peasant militia and in creating an institutional order, the whole country has been prey to continual anarchic violence, with no meaning; each party simply matching the excesses of the adversary (whether Liberal or Conservative) with excesses of its own, without coherence or leadership. . . .

"The problem of political power was only confronted in 1964 by the peasant guerilla of Marquetalia, which articulated a serious organization, objectives, and a phased programme, in short a meaning for itself."

The violence clearly created a problem for the Communists when a few years ago both Moscow and Peking began to press for Communists in countries like Colombia to begin to raise guerilla armies with a view to some day, probably after a long and protracted struggle, seizing power as Castro had done.

The Communists of Guatemala and Venezuela, as I have noted, answered the call by establishing insurrectionary bases in mountain areas. The problem for Colombia's Communists was that there were tens of thousands of guerilla fighters of a sort already established in those very areas where they might be expected most easily to get a following for their own guerilla bands. But the existing guerillas had discredited guerilla warfare by letting it degenerate into senseless killing and banditry. Nonetheless, the Communists decided to try to win the best of the bandits over to Communism and so provide them with an ideology for which to fight.

They have had some success in this. A few weeks before my arrival in Colombia in 1965 one of the best known of the bandit leaders had declared himself a convert to Marxism. In this case he did not claim to be a Communist party member, nor did the Communists claim him as such. But they hailed his conversion to the cause of the workers, and the probability is that both felt that discretion demanded that he should not declare himself a Communist even if in fact he had become one. The Communist press today gives support to the bandits, and condemns their "repression" by the government. This involves constantly walking a tightrope.

At any moment a group of bandits somewhere, not necessarily connected in any way with the Communists, may be guilty of some appalling atrocity with which the Communist party has no desire to be associated. During my stay in Colombia, bandits held up a bus crammed with innocent rural people and decapitated every one of them, men, women, and children alike. Since this incident was a widely publicized one, the party appears to have decided to brazen it out. Before long, sickening photographs of the decapitated victims were going up on city walls with captions which suggested that government troops had been responsible for the outrage.

I ask left-wing students how they could possibly support a movement which was in any way associated with atrocities like this.

The campesinos, they said, had been degraded by illiteracy and poverty. The atrocities simply emphasized the need to sweep away a capitalist system which could so degrade the poor, and they underlined for them the need to win over the bandits to Marxism. Their rich experience of guerilla warfare might then be turned to the service of humanity instead of being wasted in the pitiless killing of each other and of members of their own class.

As in Venezuela, most of Colombia's Communist groups now support urban terrorism, too. The number of bombings and kidnappings has increased steadily month by month. Some of those responsible for them have undoubtedly been common criminals, for lawlessness is in any case on the increase. But the few people who have been caught with bombs have in the main been young students. The Communists, however, put around the story that the military were responsible for the terrorism and had faked this campaign so that they could blame it on the Communists and thus justify a military coup.

During one period when the guerillas were much in the news, advertisements offering arms for sale to the general public, and inserted by the army, appeared in the local press. It seemed extraordinary that the government of a country in which large numbers of guerillas were in the process of being welded into a revolutionary force under Communist leadership should suddenly offer arms to all and sundry.

I discussed this with a general whose answer was revealing. The forces of law and order, he said, were quite incapable of controlling urban crime and violence. Recent kidnappings in which huge ransoms had been demanded of wealthy families had led to demands for a degree of protection which the government could not provide. This being so, the only way in which their minds could be put at rest was to enable them to arm themselves. Well-to-do citizens had also organized their own civil defense committees for the protection of their lives and property, and these too were now able to arm themselves with the obsolete weapons of which the army was disposing.

But, I persisted, would not the guerillas take advantage

of the same offer and so become an even greater problem?

There was, he replied, no fear of this since the bandits and the Communist-led guerillas already had far more arms than they required and these were of as good and better quality than those possessed by the army itself.

The night I met Father Camillo Torres Restrepo in Bogota he was so taut that it was obvious that he was in the process of taking some decision which was costing him a very great deal. A few days later he took to the hills. Not long after, early in 1966, he was shot to death by government forces while leading a guerilla band.

The 37-year-old rebel priest, chaplain to Bogota University, came of a well-to-do family. He studied sociology at Louvain University and in the United States. His interest in social questions was quickened and fed by the contrast between his own social background and that of his country's poor. He found it impossible to understand his ecclesiastical leaders' prudence and caution when faced with monstrous social injustices which were degrading so many, driving others, the good as well as the bad, into armed rebellion and which seemed to cry aloud to heaven for vengeance.

His country's bishops had issued strongly worded calls for agrarian reform and a crusade for the liberation of the rural population, but the Church's identification with the oligarchy, which he knew all too well, outraged him. The rural and urban poor, who were his great preoccupation, were thrown by a fast deteriorating economic situation into a head-on clash with the very forces with which the Church still had close and damaging links.

Discussing these things late into the night with the students among whom he worked and who themselves frequently came from a background of poverty, he moved farther and farther to the Left. Although condemned as a Communist (I was warned against him as soon as I arrived in the country), he never became a Marxist. And although he spoke out against what he regarded as the failure of his ecclesiastical superiors to denounce in clear terms the Colombian oligarchy and the United States domination of his country, he defended the Church in other matters.

"The temporal defects of the Church should not scandalize us," he said. "The Church is human. The important thing to believe is that it is also divine, and that if we Christians fulfill the obligation to love our neighbor we are strengthening the Church." His refusal to say Mass, in the period leading up to his becoming a guerilla priest, sprang from a sincere desire to share the isolation and rejection of the poor and, in particular, of the revolutionaries who are their champions.

Father Camillo's decision to join the guerillas was in itself an indication that among them today are authentic revolutionaries who have rebelled against real injustices and are prepared to die for genuine ideals. The day when Colombia's insurgent bands could be dismissed as exclusively composed of blood-thirsty, sadistic bandits is gone. This would seem to indicate that the Communists know what they are doing when they send their members to join them with a view to converting the movement to the revolutionary cause.

Father Camillo's life and death, tragic though they were, are also a reminder that in the ranks of the younger clergy in particular there are men today who, even though they do not go as far as he did, are determined to make theirs the Church of the poor.

During the civil war which dragged on for 10 years, a number of so-called "independent republics" were formed in various parts of Colombia. Independent republics have a long history in Colombia and grow out of the nature of the terrain. Traditionally peasants in remote and almost totally isolated mountain areas have from time to time refused to accept the fiat of the central government, then set up their own administration and defended themselves with arms against any attempt to subdue them.

Between 1948 and 1958 such centers of resistance were established in Marquetalia, Rio Chiquito, Sumapaz, El Pato. Those responsible were nominally Liberal supporters, involved in the nationwide fight with the Conservatives. In fact, since these were areas of enormous poverty and land hunger, local risings were much more in the nature of peasant revolts than struggles in support of a political party.

When the war officially ended, the peasant leaders, among whom were by now some members of the Central Committee of the Communist Party, advised their followers not to put down their arms, but to proclaim these "liberated areas" as independent republics. These have become centers of guerilla activity. Marquetalia and El Pato, in particular, have the direct and continuous support of Castro's radio, and occasional reference is made to them by Radio Moscow and Radio Peking.

The army, assisted by its U.S. advisers, has from time to time made attempts to destroy the independent republics. They have met with only limited success. Even when the operations have appeared to achieve their purpose, it is usually found that the guerillas have taken to the surrounding hills and from there they subject the army to continuous harassment until it is driven out again. Marquetalia is a natural fortress since it is accessible only through a narrow canyon. It is difficult, therefore, to conduct an assault against it.

Castro's successful revolution undoubtedly inspired many of those who provide the new political leadership of the guerillas in these independent republics and elsewhere. But Moscow-line and Peking-line leaders have also joined them, and in these conditions they seem so far to work together reasonably well.

It is the "Fidelistas" (followers of Castro), pro-Peking Communists, and Left Socialist revolutionaries who place the main emphasis upon the armed struggle and who therefore show the greatest enthusiasm for the work among the guerillas and in the independent republics. As was formerly the case in Venezuela, the Moscow-line Communist leadership finds itself obliged to support them if it is not to forfeit forever its claim to be a revolutionary party. It has to provide positive proof of the falsity of Peking's jibe that pro-Moscow Communist parties are "anti-imperialist in word, pro-imperialist in deed." But it insists that the armed and constitutional struggles must be integral parts of the same movement and that both must go forward together.

A plenary meeting of the party's leaders, held in March, 1965, adopted a statement which made its position plain. The country's most reactionary circles were, it declared, openly asking for "Yankee military intervention against the guerilla movement and the various manifestations of growing popular discontent."

It went on: "Operation Marquetalia has been followed by military invasions with air transport, such as those in El Pato, and preparations for aggression against other peasant areas are on foot with the most active co-operation of the North American military missions.

"These facts have led to a new stage in the guerilla struggles in our country. The struggles are spreading because new *foci* have developed and are giving rise to a guerilla movement which is growing day by day and which is a special factor in the national political perspective.

"In the areas attacked under the official policy of blood and fire and with the pretext of exterminating so-called 'independent republics', the guerilla action has been converted into the principal method of struggle of the peasant masses. The prospects for development of the guerilla movement are linked, nevertheless, to the whole complex of the political situation and to the furtherance of the actions of the masses in the cities, in the proletarian centers, and among the workers in the country.

"The Communist party reiterates its position, viz., that it considers just the form of armed struggle as expressed in peasant and popular resistance against official aggression. This resistance can survive and increase if it retains the active support of the masses and if it stimulates its own unity and that of the popular forces in all their aspects. . . ."

Among delegates to the Communist party's Congress held in early 1966 were ones with credentials from guerilla units. The Congress recognized that the guerilla struggle had been forced upon the movement at a time "when Colombia is not experiencing a revolution and no general insurrection is possible due to the 'fire and sword' policy pursued by the reactionaries. . . ." Nonetheless "the gue-

A Venezuelan child and her sister outside their "ranchito"
overlooking Caracas.

A twelve year old boy scavenges through the city dump of a small barriada on the outskirts of Lima. On his burro he transports bottles, metal and other scrap items that he can sell.

rilla struggle in a number of areas benefits the masses and harmonizes with the aspirations of the people."

In the month of February, 1967, alone, terrorist attacks cost the lives of 30 soldiers. Their activities during the following month included the use of machine guns and dynamite in raids on trains. And so it goes, with government attacks upon the guerillas and reprisals by terrorists against both military and civilians.

In the conditions which exist in Colombia, even the Moscow-line Communist party can hold out no prospect of using parliamentary democracy in the way that its sister party in Chile has done in recent years.

Among the student bodies in the universities, which are the Communists' other strongholds, rivalry between the various Marxist groups has begun to weaken their total impact. In the University of Bogota, for example, eight different student groups calling themselves "Marxist" and "revolutionary" contend for leadership of the student body. One is pro-Moscow; another, pro-Peking; a third, pro-Castro. Then there are pro-Moscow-and-Castro and pro-Peking-and-Castro groups, a Trotskyist one, and a few Leftist Marxist-Leninist organizations owing allegiance to neither Russia, Peking, nor Cuba. As in Caracas, there are times when it would appear that they are fighting each other more fiercely than they are fighting the capitalist enemy.

THE CHURCH ORGANIZES ITSELF

In striking contrast to the growing fragmentation of the Communist movement stands CELAM (*Consejo Episcopal Latinoamericano*—Council of Latin American Bishops), a Bogota-based organization which is coordinating the work of the bishops throughout the entire Latin American sub-continent. It is unique among Church organizations anywhere.

The mere fact of CELAM's existence is an indication of a willingness on the part of the bishops as a group to put themselves on the side of change and to attempt to bring the whole of Latin America into the twentieth century. It would, of course, be a gross exaggeration to suggest that every bishop from Mexico to the southernmost tip of South America is now eager to be in the forefront of the Latin American revolution. But the creation of CELAM in 1956 and its recent reorganization reflects an acknowledgement on the part of the majority of bishops of the need for new thinking and planning, new attitudes and new activities.

It is a tacit recognition of the fact that the Church was falling behind in this age of change; that while the rest of the world was moving forward, the Church was at best standing still and most probably moving backward; and that the answer to this is not simply to try to catch up with the rest, but rather to be giving a lead to others.

CELAM assists the Church to think and plan on a continental scale. This not only represents an important break with its own past, but with what is still the prevailing tendency of most Latin Americans to think in terms of their own country rather than in continental terms.

The practice, as elsewhere, has been for each bishop to think within the context of the relatively narrow confines of his own diocese, rather as though the bishops were the rulers of so many autonomous republics, each existing in isolation from the rest. He thought and planned in diocesan terms. At the best, the bishops of any particular country thought collectively in national terms.

CELAM is not some sort of High Command, able to dictate to bishops what they should or should not do. It does not make decisions binding on them all. Nor does it even directly initiate or promote ideas. Its purpose is the coordination of ideas. But the very act of exchanging ideas and experiences can encourage new ones. It can also lead to their being translated into actions.

An example of how this works may be drawn from its Social Action Service Department which, so far, has probably been the least used of the ten departments through which CELAM works.

A bishop who wishes to issue a pastoral letter on a social question will today most probably first get in touch with CELAM's director at its headquarters in Bogota, or directly with CELAM's Social Action Department. These will then supply the necessary background material and in addition provide information about pastoral letters issued by other bishops on the same subject.

Another may, perhaps, wish to issue a pastoral which is intended to give a lead on the need for agrarian reform. Again he is likely to turn to CELAM and so insure that his letter shall be based upon the realities, taking into account both possibilities and potential pitfalls. A third may want to know more about the formation of producers' cooperatives and credit unions by Church organizations. CELAM will be able to provide all the information required. In due course this is used to stimulate appropriate action.

Such requests come to CELAM in a steady stream. And the more the inquiries come, the more the Church goes into action all over the sub-continent.

In the past, a bishop who launched out, possibly with a good deal of misgiving, into some new form of social action did so in isolation. He knew little of what others were doing. Most probably they never heard of the initiative he had taken.

When the Mexican bishops were considering starting a radio adult education scheme, CELAM was able to provide them with all the information they required about the *Escuelas Radiófonicas* in Colombia, and similar projects elsewhere. On several occasions recently, bishops in countries where there are large Indian populations, among whom no work in the social field has hitherto been done, have got in touch and been advised accordingly. They have been put in contact with people qualified to get right on with the work at once.

CELAM has made a special study of the various UN and other international organizations working in Latin America so that bishops who wish to make the fullest possible use of them can be given the necessary guidance. The planning of the work of the Papal Volunteers, and other lay mission helpers from the United States, has also become one of its functions.

This constant interchange of experience as between one country and another is doing an immense amount to create a continental outlook within the Church. This actually places it ahead of the politicians who in the main still tend to think in terms of their own particular countries and their needs, rather than on a continental scale.

When it was first set up, the whole work and organization of CELAM was concentrated at the headquarters in Bogota. More recently both have been decentralized. Ten departments, each presided over by a bishop, have been established. Between them they cover every aspect of the Church's work. Those who head these departments are in practically every case among the most progressive and certainly the most go-ahead. The various departments have headquarters in different parts of Latin America. They aim to coordinate the activities of the various organizations already existing in their own particular field, to learn from them, and to make known their experiences to others. Each department is assisted by experts drawn from countries all over Latin America.

Because of the changes in the liturgy introduced by the Second Vatican Council, one of the busiest of the ten is the liturgical department. Generally speaking, it may be said that the bishop whose mind is opened to the need for changes in a long-established liturgy will also be receptive to changes in other directions.

The Education Commission draws upon Dutch and French expertise and avails itself of what UNESCO and other international organizations have to offer. It is nonetheless trying to think along distinctively Latin American lines to ensure that, as education programs go forward, they shall not simply be copies of schemes which have succeeded in other areas with different problems, but shall be adapted to Latin American needs. Some of its work may well prove to be of great value to other countries where conditions may be similar—particularly in the mission areas of Asia and Africa.

"We need an education of development as well as a development of education," says Father Isaac Wüst, the Dutch priest who runs the education department. But, of course, to have an educational system which is geared to the needs of a developing country, one must also have specialized knowledge of economic planning, industrial development, rural development, urban and rural needs, and

much more besides. Thus the work of the education department, linked through CELAM with the work of the social
action and other departments, leads on to a recognition of
the need for a Christian interest in every aspect of life.

The sessions of the Vatican Council have shown, as one
would expect, that among the bishops of Latin America are
traditionalists and progressives, those who welcome change
and those who are nervous about it or may even resist it.
Contrary to what is often thought outside of Latin America, by now, if one can put bishops into various camps,
Latin America probably has fewer "last-ditch," confirmed
traditionalists than Europe.

One man who works very closely with the bishops told
me that he considered that not more than ten per cent can
now be described as die-hard traditionalists; another ten
per cent he would class as progressives, prepared to consider
the merits of anything new. The other 80 per cent, when
confronted with any particular situation, instinctively tend
first to think along traditional lines, but then in practice
follow the progressives if given a decisive lead.

Latin America's traditionalists are challenged at every
turn. What they all know today is that Latin America must
change, and that the change must be a radical one. The
word *revolution* is on everyone's lips, no matter whether
they discuss social, economic, or industrial matters. The psychology of Latin America is the psychology of a continent
in change.

If the bishops come to think in these terms—as increasing numbers are already doing—then they will be disposed
to think of change in the Church too. And from this, experience shows, they more easily go on to accept the need
for social change.

For this reason CELAM's rôle may well become increasingly important with every year. The scope and pace of its activities are likely to grow as more and more change occurs in the thinking of the bishops whom it serves, while at the same time it will itself be influencing that process.

Agrarian Reform, Shanty Towns, and Indians

In his office in Lima, Héctor Cornejo Chávez, President of Peru's Christian Democrat party, talked to me of the need for agrarian reform, Latin America's most pressing problem.

In Peru, as elsewhere in Latin America, he said, one of the inescapable facts of the situation is the unjust distribution of wealth in general and of land in particular. He quoted the example of the coastal region—the country's richest—in which 180 persons own 56 per cent of the area under cultivation.

The same sort of situation, but in more dramatic form, is found in the mountain and jungle regions. "So we have little groups with a high standard of life and culture," he said, "and a vast mass of people existing within the same country with appallingly low standards." Then, striking what by now was a familiar note, he added: "That is why Christian Democrats tell you so often that we must change the whole structure of society. Nothing less than a profound, deep transformation is required."

Although Peru's Christian Democrats are not yet as strong as Venezuela's, they had entered their country's government, albeit as the smaller partner, whereas Rafael Caldera and his party were in opposition. Héctor Cornejo Chávez told me that his party had followed this course so that they might learn something of the art of government, for they, like their sister party in Venezuela, were convinced that Eduardo Frei's success in Chile had brought the possibility of a victory much nearer—indeed, they regarded a victory at the next elections, in 1969, as not impossible.

The senior partners in Peru's government were the *Apristas*, members of APRA—*Alianza Popular Revolucionaria Americana*—whose elderly leader Víctor Raúl Haya de la Torre has lost much of that fire in his belly which once made him known as a revolutionary all over Latin America. Despite the fact that it is living on its past, APRA still syphons off some of the revolutionary tendencies among students which might otherwise go to the Communists. But as Haya de la Torre and the other leading *Apristas* have become more "respectable" and less and less adventurous, so the Christian Democrats in the government have assumed the rôle of the ones who demand new approaches.

They note perhaps a little wistfully that in Chile the bishops watched the activities of the Christian Democrats with sympathy and understanding and, by giving a bold lead on the most urgent social problems, helped to create the climate of opinion which enabled the party to come to power. This is not the situation in Peru, where the majority of Church leaders still tend to be traditionalists.

In Chile, the Church gave the lead in agrarian reform and set an example by "reforming" its own land. The Church in Peru has far less land today than at the time of the liberation when she was said to have owned one-third of all the country's property. All too much of this went, if the truth be told, in shameful ways, with priests selling it to buy gifts for their concubines or leaving it to their sons. But some of the dioceses and religious orders still rank as big landowners.

In some cases, they have given their land for reform, but not in all. "It is said," one Christian Democrat told me, "that Pope Paul takes the view that the disadvantages which come from the Church's owning land far outweigh the advantages and that he would be glad to see the Church part with the last square inch. But the message seems not to have got through to some of the bishops and religious superiors here in Peru." Critics within the Church say that the bishops back the land reform as an idea, but are so convinced that they need their lands to support their work that in practice they fail to give the leadership which others expect of them.

Héctor Cornejo Chávez talked of Peru's agrarian reform which some would claim to be, on paper at least, one of the best in Latin America. The reform was promoted by his party, but was hacked about by Parliament and finished up as something less than the Christian Democrats had hoped for. "We would like it to be more audacious," he said. "But we can make a start from it." The reform was at that time only one year old, and the government was still at the stage where it was discovering just how many thousands of peasants remained on a purely feudal basis. The next step would be to give 20,000 of them the title deeds which mean so much to them.

The passion of the Latin American peasant for title deeds is, incidentally, so strong that in Bolivia there are landowners who years ago were dispossessed of much of their land under the land reform, but who to this day turn a dishonest penny by selling title deeds to the very peasants to whom their land was given.

Dr. Javier Silva Ruete, Peru's 29-year-old Christian Democrat Minister of Agriculture, was a living proof that, should elections bring his party to power, it would not be lacking in talent when it came to forming a government.

There are in Peru a few enormous estates which are highly mechanized and very efficient. These, the Minister told me, will not be touched by the land reform. To submit them to a process of fragmentation would be a retrogressive step and would seriously affect the country's economy. But there is a much larger number which are quite needlessly unproductive. Their owners simply have more land than they can be bothered with. Enough is cultivated to maintain the landowner and his family in the luxury to which they are accustomed. The rest of the land goes uncultivated, while land-hungry peasants living around it suffer from chronic malnutrition for want of the food which it might produce. These estates will be broken up. The State will give an initial, fixed down payment. The remainder of the price of the land will be spread over a period of from 18 to 20 years, with payment made in shares in projects for industrial development. By this means a transfer of capital is achieved from the rural to the industrial sector.

The method used by the government when valuing land due for reform deliberately penalizes the dishonest and inefficient landowner. The price which must be accepted by the landowner is, as the Minister put it to me, based on three facts: 1) the tax which has been paid in the past by the landowner—in other words if he has been a tax dodger, deliberately writing down the value of his land, he will now suffer accordingly; 2) the value placed on the land in its present condition by surveyors acting on behalf of the State; and 3) the potential productivity of the land. "We add the three together and then divide by three." This clearly discriminates, not unjustly, against precisely the sort of landowners who have made a reform so urgently necessary.

But the agrarian reform does not simply involve a redistribution of privately owned land. Taking the long view, much more important than the distribution of private land may be the distribtuion of state-owned land which is at present unproductive. More than 60 per cent of Peru is jungle, much of it mountainous, but often nonetheless very fertile. The government proposes by 1969 to develop one million hectares of this land.

A necessary prelude to such jungle clearance is the building of roads. This has been made the Army's responsibility and has already begun. Once the roads are made and the jungle is cleared, people from the land-hungry areas will be moved in. If the agrarian reform is fully carried into practice, it will involve a mass migration within Peru's own borders and a vast development of areas at present totally undeveloped.

Will these ambitious plans be carried into effect, or will most of them remain forever on paper? That is the question which Jorge Velásquez, Secretary-General of the Christian peasant union, *Movimento Sindical Cristiano del Peru* ("MOSICP"), was asking when I discussed the reform with him. Peru's Christian Democrat movement, like the Christian Democrat party of Italy, draws support from both Left and Right, with its supporters linked by religious rather than ideological ties. Jorge Velásquez, a militant young Negro, was moulded and formed by the *Jocists* (Young Christian Workers movement). He and his peasant union are in the party's Left wing.

Jorge has led demonstrations of shoeless *campesinos* into Lima to urge that the land reform be more quickly made a reality. He has even gone on a hunger strike to support this demand. He is impatient, but so too are the 200,-000 supporters he claims among the half-starved Indians and the rural poor.

In the positions of power within the Christian Democrat party, he complains, are great landowners who use land reform as a political slogan and who would be terrified if they found it being applied to themselves. The first thing the big coffee grower who backs the Christian Democrats asks when people start talking seriously about land reform is, "What is going to happen to my 18,000 hectares?"

Much of this is an understandable expression of the frustration Jorge feels as he sees the poverty of his land-hungry people and has to watch the reform necessarily beginning with months of paper work and the laborious legal processes of getting title deeds to the dispossessed. For him, the fight for land and for agrarian reform is a crusade for justice on behalf of those who have traditionally suffered nothing but injustice. "We not only want agrarian reform," he says, "we want political power, we want economic development, social conditions which will let the poor, who are the sons of God, feel as though they are the sons of God. With the reconquest of the soil we shall change the rest of society."

INDIAN OUTSIDERS

The Indians are in the main the poorest of the rural poor. The injustices they suffer go back a long way. The rebellions and wars of independence led by Simón Bolívar and other Latin American liberators a century and a half ago appeared progressive in their time. But they left the condition of the Indians largely unchanged.

Latin American colonial society was a highly stratified one, but it was divided into two main groups. First, there were the Spaniards and Creoles—people of Spanish or mixed blood, born in Latin America. Second, there were the Indians, whom Spanish colonial civilization hardly touched. The educational and legal system, everything that went to make up Latin American society, was confined to the first group. The Indians had their own, quite different, legal system which the Spaniards continued to use for them; they were denied all education. The wars of liberation from Spain were "settlers' revolts." In this respect they were not unlike the revolt of the Rhodesian white settlers against the British government in 1965. With independence, the Creoles were freed, but the Indians remained as before.

The Indians to this day, despite their numbers, are still a group outside Latin American civilization. Even though the overwhelming majority of Peruvians have some Indian blood in their veins, the Indians are still as neglected as were their forefathers. Of 6,000,000 Indians, some 4,000,-000 do not speak Spanish, the language of those who call themselves Peruvian. Since they have practically no cash income and are outside the money economy, they cannot pay taxes and so are obliged to give work in lieu of taxes, thus retaining some of the characteristics of feudal serfs.

Though many of the Indians are devoted to the superstitious practices of the pre-Christian era, they think of themselves as Christians. And, quite simply, they accept Jorge's leadership because they know him to be the spokesman of a Christian peasant union. For the same reason, they frequently refuse to give a hearing to the Communists who come hoping to organize them for a "revolutionary solution to the land problem," but who they know are opposed to all religion.

If Peru's agrarian reform is fully put into practice, the jungle and mountain areas where the Indians live will be opened up, the standard of life of the rural people will rise, and they will be brought into the money economy of the towns. The gap between the two civilizations will at last be bridged. But something more dynamic than a coalition dominated by a party which long ago exhausted its revolutionary potentialities will be required to make all this a reality.

The Christian Democrats will probably have to acquire more of an ideology than they have at this moment if their party is to be given any cohesion and the will to lead the social revolution of which they talk. The stresses and strains between Left and Right wings are already considerable. Nonetheless, the experience of Chile shows that a recognition of the challenge of the Marxist Left can awaken the traditionalists to the likelihood that, unless they are prepared to bring their thinking into the twentieth century, they will disappear as a class.

RURAL DYNAMITE

Land is dynamite in Latin America today. Without genuine agrarian reform, which means the bringing of the rural areas and their people out of feudalism and into the modern age, even industrial development must fail to result in the creation of a healthy economy and a just social system.

In every country of Latin America there is too much land in the hands of the few, too little in the hands of the many. It has been said that in Chile and Brazil, two per cent of the population owns 50 per cent of the workable land. In Venezuela, three per cent of the population owns 90 per cent of the land. In general, in Latin America, with the exception of Mexico and Cuba, five per cent of the population owns half of the land. Nothing can justify such a situation. It leads to a failure to use natural resources to their full, to low productivity, rural unemployment, and a drift from the land to the cities; and this creates an almost insoluble urban problem too. There can be no question of Latin America's being brought into the twentieth century until agrarian reforms get off the drawing board and into practice.

A succession of Catholic Rural Life conferences held throughout the '50s in various parts of Central and South America contributed to putting the Church in the forefront of the demand for agrarian reform. On this many of the bishops can with justice claim to have been among the first to speak out, even though some may have done it somewhat hesitantly.

Fairly typical was a joint statement issued by the Colombian bishops in 1960 calling for agrarian reform and a crusade for the liberation of the rural population. Land reform cannot be achieved overnight, it stressed. "Serious and intense study" would be needed before it could begin. Reform should proceed in a "slow transformation," without demagogic pressure or unjust expropriation. Colombia's bishops are not the continent's most progressive or adventurous. Yet even so they were helping to create a public opinion in favor of land reform where practically none existed before.

Land redistribution was necessary, they wrote, to correct present injustices and to make the use of land conform to the common good. The concentration of land in the hands of a few could be anti-social. So, too, could holdings so small as to be uneconomic. So both extremes must be corrected. Farm workers' wages were too low; farm rents, too high; and the share-cropping system was unjust. Simple land redistribution was not enough. Along with it, there must be provision for agricultural credit at reasonable interest. Health, irrigation, and drainage projects needed to be initiated, and farmers needed to be able to get an integrated education.

Several of the men who have been responsible for the land and agrarian reforms in Latin American countries were delegates years ago to the Catholic Rural Life conferences which were promoting what was at that time an unpopular cause. This was true in the case of Venezuela which was among the first in the field. The Christian Democrat Minister of Agriculture in Betancourt's government got a land reform on the statute books with which few social reformers could quarrel. But the great landed interests delayed its implementation and in the early years came near to reducing it to farce. One could drive for miles along a road bordered by a single estate whose fertile soil was producing luxuriant crops; the soil would thin; the crops would become poorer; and then would come a Ministry of Agriculture notice proclaiming that this land had been redistributed under the terms of the new land laws. This distortion of the purposes of the land reform is not so blatant today. But no one could pretend that the reform has brought the rural revolution which was intended. It has a long way to go before it nears completion and still farther before its social aims are realized.

The same may be said of one Latin American country after another. This represents not merely a defeat of the purposes of government; it is a story of hopes raised and dashed—on the part of people who have never before dared hope for anything in this life. The danger is that this will lead to disillusionment, bitterness, or a return to an even more total apathy than before.

SHANTY TOWNS

When I was in Pusan at the end of the Korean War, I wrote that I had never seen housing conditions more degrading than those I found there. I had not at that time seen the slums of Lima. When, shortly afterward, I did so, I had to acknowledge that here were conditions just as bad as those I had found in the great Oriental port, but with this difference: Pusan's housing problem had been immensely aggravated by a war situation, but Lima's *barriadas* (shanty towns) were in danger of being accepted as normal, even though they were every bit as bad as Pusan's. I was later to see the *callampas* of Santiago de Chile and the *favelas* of Rio de Janeiro and to realize that such shanty towns are a feature of practically every great Latin American city. But Lima's are probably the most extensive of any. They have also got most attention from the American press. Yet I have talked to people living in the city's fashionable suburbs who hardly know of their existence and who refuse to believe that they can be as bad as they are. Others know of their existence, but do everything they can to discourage visitors from seeing them or writing about them because, they claim, "it is bad for Peru." There is no quick and easy solution to the problem of Lima's shanty towns. The important thing is that their existence should be understood, and faced.

Lima, like every other Latin American city and, for that matter, most other great cities throughout the world, has always had its slums. But a new situation has been created in recent years by a two-way movement of the population. From the mountain and jungle belts have come wave upon wave of Indians driven from their homes by famine, crop failure, or because they can no longer endure the degrading poverty and malnutrition into which they were born. This movement of population is part, also, of the great drift from the land which is almost universal today. But it is not just a question of the bright city lights attracting a rural population. Sheer starvation drives them as well. As a consequence, the migration from the land to the city takes dramatic forms.

On one occasion, five thousand people moved into the outskirts of Lima from the hinterland in a single night. One more vast new slum had been created between sunset and daybreak. In fairness to the Peruvian authorities one may say that neither New York, London, nor Hamburg, despite all their affluence, could easily cope with such a problem.

When they arrive, the people from the hills and jungles proceed to erect shacks for themselves. Since Lima never has rain (and, its people complain, it never has sun either), roofs are not essential. The new shacks are built of cardboard, old sacking and matting, flattened-out kerosene cans. When possible, the newcomers settle around a river which will then be their bath, their sewer, and their water supply merged into one. They have neither lighting, cooking facilities, water, or sewerage. To the best of my knowledge no one has ever done a careful study of how they survive. Somehow they manage to exist by the odd cent earned here and there and on scraps of food found by their children in the more prosperous parts of the town. One may well argue that their last state is worse than their first, yet they still continue to come. There are probably half a million such people squatting on the outskirts of Lima today.

The migrants from the mountains and jungles are joined by people who leave the old slums and city center for the new ones on its periphery. This is a very Latin American thing to do. In the old urban slum they are dependent on the landlord, hemmed in by restrictions. Despite the lack of facilities in the new slum, those who live in it have a certain independence. There is no landlord. Ramshackle as the new shanty may be, it is something that a man has built for himself. He has made it. He owns it.

When I first saw Lima's barriadas years ago, I too readily concluded that the problem they presented was so huge that there could be little hope of its being solved either by government or by the people themselves. I was wrong. After an absence of eight years, I returned to Lima's barriadas. I asked to be taken to those I knew. The houses were still too small by any standards, immensely too crowded. They had been built on a wasteland which still looked like a wasteland. But the cardboard, matting, and tin shanties had been converted into little stone houses. In the streets there were standpipes; in some cases the water supply had been taken right into the people's homes. There was electric light. Some was, admittedly, illegally "borrowed"; for at night hundreds, maybe thousands, connect their houses to overhead cables. Others had lighting systems legally installed, with the current paid for in the normal way. Some of the roads, which had been practically open sewers, were now surfaced. The people had a pride in their homes and in their neighborhood.

By Lima's standards, the "hopeless" slums I had seen on my first visit had become little working-class and lower middle-class suburbs. Sociologists have discovered that behind the ant-like activity of the barriada, where each man would appear to be busy solving only his own problems, there is an extraordinary amount of social organization. Traditionally, in the countryside, they built their homes together, planted crops together, harvested them together. There was a community existence. This is carried over into the barriada. It is the people themselves who by their organization solve many of their problems.

They have been assisted by selfless priests who have gone to live among them. The Irish Columban Fathers have done a magnificent job in this. It was they who first introduced me to Lima's vast new slums. They knew them well, for they themselves were living in them, sharing the life of the people. When I went back to them in 1965, the slum parish in which I had formerly stayed was now an established and respectable suburb. But other Columban Fathers were working in new barriadas which extended miles beyond the old ones and which were just as primitive as these had been a few years earlier.

In one of the worst, built around a smouldering, stinking municipal garbage heap, lives Father Louis Dineen, a young Irish Columban. He lives and works in a vast area of newly-erected shacks and unmade-up roads, of hundreds of starving stray dogs, of noise, squalor, and social misery. But already he had brought many of his people into an organization which had negotiated with the Christian Democrat Mayor of Lima to have electricity brought into the *barriada*. The process of going up the ladder from degradation to dignity had begun.

The shanty town problem is clearly one which cannot be solved in isolation. It is inextricably bound up with rural poverty. The flight from the land is unlikely to end so long as rural conditions are such that even the *barriadas* seem good by comparison. The new urban populations cannot be absorbed until there is more industrial development. The process of making the slums less degrading, less dehumanizing, can only be accelerated when a social conscience —which can most easily come from the Church—has been created among the population as a whole.

Lima's *barriadas* are out of sight. They are not on the road to anywhere. The consequence is that the people of Lima itself may not even see the contrast between the city's richest and poorest. There is no escaping this contrast in Caracas, and the provocation there is correspondingly greater. Caracas has what must surely be the most luxurious army officers' club in this world. And, quite literally, just across the road some of the worst slums in this world creep up the hillside on to which the windows of the club look out. You cannot travel far round Rio de Janeiro without seeing the *favelas* rising tier upon tier up the sides of the hills which were once the city's glory and are now its shame. In this twentieth century one just cannot have blatant contrasts like these, extremes of wealth and poverty existing side by side, without sooner or later having a social up-heaval of some sort.

Students had been burning buses in the streets of Lima shortly before I got there. This is a form of protest popular in most developing countries and a steady favorite throughout Latin America. There is, it seems, a peculiar satisfaction about seeing a bus go up in flames, quickly to be reduced to a useless metal skeleton. Few protests bring visible results. Here is one that does.

The Christian Democrats are the smallest organized group among the students, but a growing one. Followers of Víctor Raúl Haya de la Torre's *Apristas* are the largest. The most militant tend to be the various Marxist groups, of whom there are at least eight competing with each other for a following in the universities. Moscow and Peking supporters fight each other so ferociously that they have lost their hold on some of the universities, although a number are still under Communist control.

The North American visitor, in particular, tends to take one look at this highly political, somewhat turbulent student mass and write it off as Communist. It is more true to say that the majority of students in Peru as, indeed, in most other Latin American countries, are first, anti-imperialist; second, anti-Yankee; third, eager to make an end of injustice. All this is expressed in lively militancy and in Left-wing terminology, but it does not necessarily add up to organized, well-understood Communism. It creates, however, a situation which a more united Communist party could effectively exploit. Those universities where the Communists are the dominant influence tend to be ones where Marxist professors predominate.

With Haya de la Torre now an old man who gives something of the impression of a burned-out volcano, it is reasonable to suppose that either the Communists or the Christian Democrats—or both—will in the years ahead attract many of the students who would formerly have gone to the *Apristas*.

There is relatively little hostility on the campus to Christianity as such. Given a lead, Christian student organizations should be able to get a growing following. But in a situation where there are only two full-time and two part-time chaplains working among 30,000 students, the majority never see the Church in its modern guise at all. They see it as an institution whose followers are identified by their adherence to fixed laws which appear to have little relevance to our day. They see it also as a powerful institution closely linked to the oligarchy and, like students all over the Western world, they are against the "establishment." Priests working among them insist that it is against the Church in these two guises that the majority of students revolt, not against the faith as such.

It is incorrect to say that the students of Peru are lost to the Church. The Church never had them. They are there to be won. But the Church has to find ways of presenting the faith in intelligent and meaningful terms. The chaplains who work among them are optimistic. Given the lead and the men, they believe that the faith may in time become a powerful, possibly the predominant force on almost every campus. But, despite Vatican Council II, there is relatively little dialogue as yet between the committed Christians and those who can only be described, for want of a better term, as non-Christians. The need for such a dialogue is often either overlooked or denied because, it is said, Peru is a Catholic country and the Peruvians, therefore, are a Catholic people.

Many priests working in Peru, as in other parts of Latin America, would feel that such terms merely conceal the true situation. It might be far better for the Church, they say, if all concerned stopped talking of "Catholic" Latin America, and if the whole sub-continent was recognized for what it is—a mission area.

THE WAKENING CHURCH

On the occasion of my first visit to Peru I looked out through the window of my aircraft as it came across the Andes. On many of the foothills I saw what appeared to be crucifixes. I told myself that it was rather like flying into Ireland. Later, I mentioned this to my host in Lima. Without comment he asked me if I would like to see some of those crosses, and in due course took me to visit them.

Situated in areas where, because of the shortage of clergy, no priests had worked for generations, they had been erected by the people, usually at the time of some natural disaster. But they were not crucifixes. There was a cross, a ladder, a bag of dice, a bag of nails, some coins—all the instruments of the Passion. One thing was missing. There was no figure on the cross. Instead there might be a bunch of evergreen leaves, denoting a mixture of tree worship and Christianity; or, maybe, a stuffed cockerel which might possibly have something to do with Peter's betrayal of Christ, but was just as likely to have more to do with witchcraft.

There had recently been a drought high in the Andes where the soil was thin and where frequent rain was essential if any crops were to survive. It had not rained for 20 months, and as a consequence some of the Indians of the area were dying of thirst, others of starvation. Those who tried to make their way through the jungle belt had in most cases gone down with diseases against which they had no natural immunities. Just before I arrived in the country, a 14-year-old girl in the region afflicted by the drought had been offered as a human sacrifice to the rain god. The only reminder that these were people who had once received something of the message of Christianity was that she had been crucified.

On another occasion I was taken to an area, one of many such, where there had been no priest for a century and a half. For generations the people had continued to celebrate the feast day of their patronal saint. The celebrations had become more and more pagan as the priestless years had gone on. Then a young priest newly out from Spain was sent to work in the area. By the time he arrived, the feast day was the one day of the year on which anyone went inside the church. And even then it was only in order to take out a huge statue of the Virgin which the men of the village carried in procession for the rest of the day. The celebrations were accompanied by an orgy of drinking and licentiousness.

The newly arrived young priest was gifted with more sincerity than wisdom. He decided that before the people were given the Mass they must get rid of this travesty of Christianity. So he told them that on the patronal feast day, which happened to fall almost immediately after his arrival, the church doors would be locked and the statue of Our Lady would remain inside. But on the following day, Mass would for the first time in generations be celebrated.

The people who crowded to the church learned that he meant what he said. To their horror he stood before the locked doors insisting that there must be no procession that day. They killed him for his pains. He appeared to be robbing them of all that was left of their Christianity.

It was in Lima that I discussed with several forward-looking Peruvian priests the impact made by the clergy who have been sent there from abroad. Spain has responded quickly and generously to the call. Will a great influx of Spanish priests make the admittedly difficult process of absorbing foreign clergy still harder? Experience has shown, I was told, that a number of seminaries in Spain are turning out dynamic, progressive young priests who have been given an excellent formation in leadership and a good knowledge of social problems. These are precisely what Latin America needs, provided that they can live down—as they may well do—the prejudice which is felt in some quarters for any priest from Spain.

Others come from groups who have failed to move with the times and whom even the bloodbath which began in 1936 in Spain did not change. The coming of these may, despite Latin America's crying need for priests, hold back rather than promote the breakthrough by the Church which is Rome's aim. Fortunately, it is the more progressive seminaries which produce the men who are most likely to respond to the demand for volunteers for Latin America. The religious orders still tend to send out priests of the old type, although this is a generalization to which there are, of course, notable exceptions.

The North American priests bring with them a businesslike practical approach, a drive, and an impatience with any tradition that stands in the way of the Church's progress. This gives their contribution a certain purgative quality urgently needed, but not necessarily always appreciated. There has frequently been a tendency on the part of North Americans to ride roughshod over Latin American sensibilities, a failure to recognize a culture which goes deeper than the culture of North America and which is more consciously appreciated by large sections of the community, a tendency, also, to take it for granted that "the American way of life" and "the free enterprise society" are somehow part of the Christian message. The bewildered Latin American often finds neither attractive.

The Germans, Dutch, French, Belgians, English, and Irish probably have less to live down than have either the priests who come from Spain or from the United States.

In practice these latter are likely to continue to come in the largest numbers, and both in practice have demonstrated—and there are many impressive examples of this—that they can not only help to fill the manpower gap, but they can also inject new life just where it is most needed.

In Peru, as in other Latin American countries, some of the local priests with the greatest drive, the keenest awareness of present requirements, and who certainly are the most outspoken, come from wealthy and influential families. This is the class which produces relatively few vocations. But when a man from such a background becomes a priest, there is a reasonable chance that he will have few inhibitions to overcome when a situation calls for frank speaking.

The process of change at work in Peruvian society does not, of course, leave the bishops untouched. The attitudes which they inherited on the social question were more concerned with remedial than preventive charity.

Tradition in Latin America is particularly strong and in the past there was little in the training and formation of the priest or the bishop to make him see beyond it. Now, as the need for something more becomes increasingly apparent, social thinking becomes more adventurous. The spirit of Vatican Council II also is at work. The consequence is that even in traditionally conservative Peru the bishops are beginning to move ahead of the land-owning class who have in the past been the all too solid pillars upon which the Church has tended to rest.

The presence of Communist guerillas in the land in 1965 and 1966 caused alarm and a sudden awareness of social problems which had for long gone unnoticed. Two members of the Peruvian hierarchy came out with statements which were in many ways remarkable. The government had conducted some fairly large-scale military operations against the guerillas and was selling bonds to finance the anti-guerilla drive. Here was something the frightened landowners could understand. Their response was immediate. But it was precisely in this situation that Peru's bishops began publicly to insist that Christianity demands something more than this, that what was really needed was sweeping social reform.

Cardinal Landazuri Ricketts, of Lima, bluntly told the rich that their luxury spending helps to spread "sentiments of desperation and rebellion" among the poor. Bishop José Dammert Bellido of Cajamarca, commenting on the rapid sale of bonds to combat the Communist guerillas, declared: "Wealthy people are not anxious to buy bonds to end social injustices. They bought bonds for the struggle against the guerillas because this is an immediate form of self-defense."

In the past, the Church has tended to identify its continued existence with the rich, but Bishop Dammert's remarks would appear to reflect a recognition that this no longer holds good today. Whomever else he did or did not expect to please by his remarks, it cannot have been Peru's wealthy citizens. He declared that he did not believe that the wealthy would assist the poor if it were not for the menace of Communism. All the country's social reforms had so far been made out of fear. The social victories had come as a result of strikes and deaths. "There has not been a true Christian conscience in Peru, and I do not believe the wealthy will aid the poor on their own initiative."

He criticized Catholic leaders and clergy who too often took a negative attitude toward social reform. The Church might not own as much land as its critics claimed, but nonetheless, he admitted, only a few of the bishops had donated their property for agrarian reform.

It is probably not too much to say that if Peru's bishops continue to be as outspoken as this, and follow words with action, regardless of the successes or failures of the Communist guerillas, then indeed will change be seen to be at work within the Church in Latin America. The effects will be felt among bishops in other Latin American countries, and in the ranks of the laity as well.

THE COMMUNISTS

Despite the fact that anti-Communists in Peru have made much of their country's Communist party, the more level-headed members of the security organizations have not in recent years generally rated either the party or its leaders very high. The party has never had a mass following, although even with a membership usually placed at somewhere around 7,000, it has still shown itself capable of working up the occasional riot when presented with suitably good "agitational issues."

All too often, in the worst, but by no means uncommon, Latin American tradition, the Communists' political opponents have been prepared to strike corrupt bargains with them, with each side using the other and knowing this to be the case. Even Conservatives have shown themselves agreeable to giving the Communists a free hand with, say, the students or workers in return for the Communists' support against a common enemy. This has resulted in the extraordinary situation where, although the Communist party has for years been illegal, it has for most of the time had a number of its members in Parliament under a variety of different labels.

The Communists have had an active and noisy following among students. There are a wide variety of rival Marxist-revolutionary and Communist groups of various kinds and differing loyalties operating in the country's universities. This obviously weakens their collective impact so far as propaganda and recruitment are concerned. Against this must be set the fact that the most active groups are the very militant pro-Peking and pro-Castro ones. In May, 1966, pro-Peking Communist students at San Marcos in Lima physically attacked those who supported Moscow. Two months later they won the student elections with the pro-Russian group falling back to third place behind the Apristas. In most parts of the country the party is a negligible force among the urban working masses, although in the south, near the Chilean border, it has for years had some genuine roots among the workers.

There was a time, some ten years ago, when it looked as though the Communist party was beginning for the first time to get a following among the rural Indians.

In the area where the Communists had their greatest success live half a million Indians, practically all illiterate. The heart of the region is Cuzco, the Incas' ancient capital. The majority of the Indians of that area are today demoralized by poverty and malnutrition. Most are addicted to chewing the narcotic coca leaf which all too frequently is issued to them by the landowners to diminish their hunger and keep them working for days on end without food.

The Communists thought that they were meeting with some success when a movement was started for those rural workers who must pay their rent to the landowner in the form of labor. At its peak, the movement embraced some 30,000 Indian peasants. An immediate setback came when, in 1961, they refused to pay the rent to the *latifundists* and troops quickly went into action against them. This show of violence soon made an end of the agitation. But the Communists lost their sympathy too because they included in their propaganda denunciation of the people's religion and superstitions. The Communists' attacks upon the practices around which the whole pattern of Indian life is built have, over the years, been resented by a people who are nothing if not religious.

Despite the greater tolerance shown toward religion by Communist parties in most parts of the world today, the Peruvian Communists and, for that matter, many of the others of Latin America, have continued in the old "sectarian" way which in the past alienated the Communists from the masses in Europe, Asia, and elsewhere.

In the early 1960s Peru's Communists, like those of

Guatemala, Venezuela, and Colombia, took to raising guerilla bands. Because the pro-Peking and pro-Castro lines
are the most popular, a surprisingly high proportion of the
Party's members have been to Cuba for training in guerilla
warfare and urban terrorism. A few have been to Peking,
and plans, which did not in the event materialize, were
being made for others to go to Algeria at the time when
Ben Bella was overthrown. A regular route which was said
to go through North Brazil was followed by the trainees.
This became known to the security authorities. Several students from good families and of outstanding promise were
among those shot when security forces attacked groups who
were making their way along this route.

In some cases, those who went abroad for training were
probably not convinced Marxists, still less were they Communist cadres. They took the opportunity for a trip to
Cuba, had an exciting experience, then returned, and because they were not at once thrown into action, tended to
drift away.

The attempt to hold the trainees by using them as
quickly as possible, coupled with pressure from Peking and
Cuba, led to a sudden growth of guerilla activity in 1965.
During the following year the security authorities conducted massive attacks upon the guerilla bases.

Régis Debray, writing in the *New Left Review* for a
Marxist public, expresses the view that the old guard Communist leaders of Peru are frankly hostile to the armed
struggle. He is probably near the truth when he writes:
"These leaders are well aware that if a 'people's war' (as
the Cubans call a guerilla war) were to break out, they
would have to yield to a new generation of leaders formed

in and by the struggle, as has happened today in Venezuela."

The Communist guerillas were, for the time being, at
least, almost destroyed as a serious threat. Only the future
will show whether they achieved anything for their cause
by their attempt to "combine armed struggle with constitutional struggle." But their mere presence in the country
was sufficient to make some people recognize the need for
reforms who might otherwise have continued to live in the
feudal past. Thus they objectively became a force for
change, even though it is not necessarily the sort of change
they as Communists desire.

And although the guerilla problem was said to have
been liquidated by the end of 1966, the social conditions
in which it had its roots remain. It may yet flare up again,
as it has already done in Venezuela.

Frei Sets the Pace

7

In September, 1964, Eduardo Frei, leader of Chile's Christian Democrat party, overwhelmingly defeated the joint Socialist-Communist candidate, Dr. Salvador Allende, in the presidential elections. Less than six months later, in the general election, Frei's party gained a working majority in the Chamber of Deputies. For the first time in this century president and parliamentary majority were both of the same party.

President Frei and the Christian Democrats gained their double victory on the basis of a political program which was hardly less revolutionary than that of Dr. Allende, their Marxist opponent.

It is not many years since Eduardo Frei was threatened with excommunication by the Church because of his political activities (with the present Pope Paul VI successfully defending him in Rome) and his party was having to fight the threat of a ban being placed on it by the Church. Nothing could better illustrate the extent and significance of the change which has occurred in Chile. President Frei's social revolution has still to come, although he has launched his country in that direction. But something of a revolution in thinking has already been achieved within the Church.

When I first visited Chile in 1957, there was little to make one suppose that in seven or eight years Chile's ecclesiastical leaders would be racing ahead of the rest of Latin America. In Santiago it was hardly reasonable to expect that the 90-year-old Cardinal would be an advocate of revolutionary change of any sort. One bishop, the late Bishop Manuel Larraín, ahead of all the rest, was already pressing for agrarian and social reform.

A few years later the bishops gave the whole movement for agrarian reform a big push forward when they carried through their own private land reform.

The workers on ecclesiastical estates were organized by the bishops into cooperatives. The land was then purchased by the cooperatives, who were given 30 years in which to pay, and divided between the individual families so that they should have a sense of private ownership while at the same time benefiting by cooperative purchasing and marketing. Where they so desired they were free to farm cooperatively too.

The bishops gave the cooperatives a little capital to get them launched and founded an institute which would concern itself with their technical and social development. In due course, Bishop Larraín of Talca was able to tell me that not only had this gesture by the Church been an act of social justice aimed at setting an example to other landowners, but that it had also proved to be economically successful. The land, under its new cooperative ownership, was producing much more than before.

With some justification Church leaders in other parts of Latin America point out that the Church in Chile was not in any case a great landowner; the extent and value of the land which was passed to the workers was not great by comparison with the huge estates owned by the Church elsewhere. The Archbishop of Santiago, for example, distributed 1,200 hectares among 150 families; the Bishop of Talca had only 180 hectares to pass over to the workers on the land.

But the significance of the bishops' private land reform in Chile was above all else a psychological one. By it, they gave a lead to other landowners. They demonstrated a practical way in which it could be done. Subsequent events have shown that, contrary to what is often claimed, it is possible to find a form of organization which results in the productivity of an estate not only being maintained, but actually increased after it has been reformed.

As the bishops went from this gesture on the land question to give leadership on many other social questions, some of the Church's critics were silenced; some even began for the first time to look to it for guidance in the search for practical answers to their country's problems. The bishops have taken to heart the first of the aims of CELAM's social action department which is "to promote the formation of social consciousness, with a view to immediate action and example from the Church, in the fulfillment of its social duties and through a testimony of poverty."

On one occasion Bishop Larraín wrote that "only one possibility exists today of improving living conditions in Latin America: a rapid and radical transformation of its economic and social institutions to bring them in line with the principles of Christian social teaching."

There emerged in Chile, just at the right moment, a group of dynamic, intelligent young Jesuits who threw their weight on the side of drastic social change. By a variety of means they spread their message far and wide, exerting their influence at levels which proved to be of decisive importance. There were priests in the slums who, also, were using their influence to create a demand for social justice.

In universities which for years had been dominated by Marxist and anti-clerical organizations new, well-led Christian organizations which modeled themselves on Cardijn's Jocists came into existence. In the University of Santiago, one group might be doing an in-depth study of the social problems of the rural people; another would be doing research into the extent and causes of alcoholism among the rural poor (one such study showed that in some areas alcoholism, growing directly out of degrading social conditions, was the greatest single killer of male adults in areas of extreme poverty).

Other groups of students went on weekends and in their vacations to live among the rural people, much as the Communist students go from Caracas into those areas where guerilla bases are being established. They taught illiterates how to read, taught the village women child-care, hygiene, dietetics. Between them they showed the people the way to a better life and helped to create a demand for it too.

Lay leaders were trained who then took both their training and their Christianity into their place of work, their trade unions, wherever they went.

Much of this activity was generated as a result of the work of the Jesuit-run *Centro Bellarmino*. Here the most intense study of social problems of any done by Catholics in Latin America is undertaken by a group of talented Jesuit priests laymen and women. The thought underlying their researches and the programs they initiate is summed up in the slogan "The social revolution must be Christianized." Father Renato Poblete, S.J., the Center's director, his famous colleague, the Belgian Father Roger Vekemans, and the team of able Jesuits working with them, set out to change the face of Chile. It is not too much to say that many of the changes that have occurred in recent years have started at *Centro Bellarmino*.

The active Christian workers in the Christian Democrat party, the unions, and the social movement consciously took from the Communists their banners, their slogans, much of their vocabulary, their campaigns against injustice, their demand for revolutionary change. This left the Communists disarmed. Christians set out to be active in all those areas of discontent in which Communism had its roots—not just in order to defeat Communism, but to create a just society. For nowhere is there a fuller recognition that Communism has grown out of the failures of Christians than among the Christian leaders of Chile.

Side by side with the growth of the Christian social movement and the ever more forceful leadership given by the bishops went the growth of the Christian Democrat party. Its leaders, like the bishops, the men at *Centro Bellarmino*, and the lay social action leaders in the Church-sponsored movement, were condemning injustice and totalitarianism, calling for social, industrial, and agrarian reform. Since their chosen field was that of politics, they conducted public campaigns for these reforms and promised the people that, if they voted them to power, they would turn principles and plans into political realities. The Church and the Christian Democrat party pursued parallel lines. But unlike parallel lines, they were converging ones.

One might say that both led to the victory of Eduardo Frei in 1964 and of his party in March, 1965.

FREI'S VICTORY

Before Frei was elected president, what has been described as a complete metamorphosis had occurred in the political thinking of Chile.

The Christians wrested the initiative on social questions from the Communists and compelled them to start thinking in different terms. In the past, the Communists had regarded the Church and Christians in politics as being suitable subjects for propagandist attacks—particularly as defenders of the *status quo*. But the Communists, looking ahead to the presidential election, were obliged to do some rethinking.

In June, 1963, the Central Committee of the Communist party, worried by the increasing clarity with which the Church was speaking out on social questions, and by the parallel growth of the Christian Democrat party's influence, discussed at length "the question of the political activity of the Church." From this Central Committee meeting came a statement which declared: "We deplore the need to concern ourselves . . . with another extremely subtle and treacherous maneuver which is being employed against the candidacy of Salvador Allende. We refer to the interference by the Church, an abuse of privilege on the part of some Church dignitaries." But the Communists recognized that the new Christian trend was not something imposed from above by the hierarchy. For Orlando Millas wrote in *World Marxist Review*: "As a matter of fact the spirit of change emanates from the parish priests who live with their parishioners in the mining villages and working-class districts and among the peasants in the villages." And despite the approaching election in which Allende (who might be described as a Chilean version of the Nenni of the 1950's) was receiving the full backing of the Communists, Millas felt obliged to admit that a joint pastoral letter of the Chilean bishops "contained justified attacks against *latifundism* and the policy of the reaction, to which they counterposed (to use their own words) "the spirituality of economic development'."

Two special issues of *Mensaje*, a Jesuit journal published in Santiago, led to a full-scale discussion of the new image and rôle of the Catholic Church by the Communist party leaders. The first special issue in December, 1962, was devoted to "The Revolution in Latin America"; the second, in October, 1963, to "Revolutionary Reforms in Latin America."

Orlando Millas wrote in an article entitled "New Trends in Catholicism and the Policy of the Chilean Communists," published in *World Marxist Review:* "The old image of the Catholic Church as implacable, intolerant, and inflexible is gradually changing. The Church, increasingly, is engaging in a dialogue, proclaiming its own rights to such values as justice and compassion, respect for human beings, for equality and progress." He described "the advent of new trends in Latin American Catholicism" as "highly significant." The Communists were worried. Millas wrote of "a reformist movement of a new type . . . a movement with a religious and theological tinge and designed to divert the Latin American revolution and frustrate it." He noted that this new "trend" dissociated itself from *latifundism* and the landed aristocracy and represented a break with the Catholic Conservative party of the past "with its feudal ties."

In May, 1965, after the Chilean elections were over, *World Marxist Review* commented:

"To stave off the inevitable setbacks, Christian Democracy has advanced a program of bourgeois reforms, designed to create a new, and more stable socio-political structure and win the masses for the 'neo-capitalist' alternative.

"A significant rôle in this has been played by the changed political orientation of the Church, which, under pressure from the Catholic masses, has adopted an anti-oligarchy attitude in recent years. It calls for an end to the 'monstrous economic inequality,' for dividing the *latifundia* among the peasants, and for a 'communitarian' society in which factory and office workers would have an equal share with the employers in running the enterprises.

"The program of the 'peaceful revolution' advocated by the Christian Democrats sounds very radical: agrarian reform which will give land to 100,000 peasants, 'Chileanization' of copper-mining, a heavy tax on capital gains, higher wages, better housing, educational reform, an independent foreign policy, trade and diplomatic relations with the socialist countries, and so on. There is no doubt that these promises reflect the interests of large sections of the working people as well as of the national and small bourgeoisie."

The Christian Democrats have insisted that theirs is not a narrowly "confessional" Christian party, still less a Catholic one. It is a party which aims to carry into effect a program of political, social, and economic reform inspired by Christian principles acceptable to any humane or progressive person—what President Frei calls a "revolution in liberty." Frei's government has in it several ministers who are outstanding and exemplary Catholics; it has also among its members some who are lapsed Catholics, free-thinkers, or agnostics, but who nonetheless find that they can give their unqualified support, not only to its aims, but to its principles as well. This is one of the many features of the new Christian Democracy which distinguish it from the Latin American Christian Democrat parties of the past which normally were Catholic in the narrowest and most exclusive sense of the word.

The major confrontation between the Popular Front of Communists and Socialists on the one hand and Christian Democrats on the other led to the Radical party, which was formerly the largest in the land, being pushed to one side. In the presidential election, Frei got 55.7 per cent of the votes, and Salvador Allende of the Popular Action Front (Socialists, Communists, and other left-wing groups) received 38.5 per cent. Julio Durán, the Radical, got only 4.9 per cent. This reflects a trend which is becoming fairly typical throughout Latin America.

The upward thrust of Christian Democracy, supported by the whole Christian social movement, and the threat of Communism, combined to push Chile's Conservatives— the political spokesmen of the traditionally Catholic moneyed and landed classes—right out of the picture by the time the elections actually took place.

There is clearly very little room for the conservatism of the past in the Chile of today. This does not, of course, mean that the traditionally conservative classes have suddenly been converted to the new Christian Democracy of Eduardo Frei, nor for that matter that they necessarily approve of the demand for social revolution made by Church leaders. It does, however, reflect the insecurity of their own position in society and their fear of Communism, particularly since Castro's victory in Cuba.

CHURCH AND PARTY

To say, as I have done, that the "converging lines" of the Church's social movement and the Christian Democrats' political struggle came together with the election of President Frei and his government is true, but only in a limited sense. It does not mean that Church and president are now hand in glove. On the contrary!

Both sides were conscious over the years of the need to provide no excuse for the charge that the Christian Democrat party was manipulated by the Church or that it was just the political arm of the Catholic hierarchy. With the coming to power of President Frei and his party, both sides have been even more scrupulously careful to avoid any entanglement with the other.

The task of the Church in the new situation, as Father Vekemans explained it to me, is to continue to keep alive and active the social conscience which has been created. Regardless of what government might be in power, this would still be necessary.

There has been a tendency for the Christian social movement to slow down because some people have imagined that the fight for social justice and Christian values has now been won. But if the social revolution is to be turned from a slogan into a fact, the need for Christian leadership is going to be greater than ever. There have been some Catholics, particularly those of the Right, who since the Christian Democrats' success at the polls, have taken the view that bishops and clergy should now go back to the sacristy. This would clearly be wrong on several counts. The very suggestion implies that their sole purpose in coming out on the social question was to make possible a victory for the Christian Democrats. And it implies that the social question may safely be left in the hands of the politicians where it properly belongs, and need no longer be regarded as the province of the Church.

The Frei government has political opportunities which no Latin American government calling itself Christian has ever had. But, like other governments, it will have to be kept up to scratch. The Church will be performing no more than its duty if it maintains a watchful guard to see, for example, that it does not take into its hands what should be the responsibility of voluntary organizations. Certainly the government itself will require an alert, vigilant, well-instructed body of Christian supporters behind it if it is not to founder within three or four years of its coming to power. For attacks upon it from both Left and Right, from the enemies of the Church and from conservative Christians, are likely to increase. The more it succeeds in its declared aim, the more will the attacks from both Right and Left build up.

Within a few months of the formation of the Frei government some of the Conservatives were beginning to get nervous. Keeping out the Communists is one thing. But to continue to support a Christian Democrat government actively intent on transforming the social structure is quite another. This requires either a Christian willingness to sacrifice personal privilege so that the underprivileged may thereby benefit, or else exceptional political sophistication.

Every minister in Frei's Cabinet whom I met during

my most recent visit was keenly conscious of this double threat which the government must increasingly face.

It is easy when one is far from Chile to suppose that the Frei administration is a one-man band, that no one else but Eduardo Frei counts for anything in the government. But this is not the situation. Frei's ministers add up to an impressive team.

DISTINCTIVE POLICIES

The Christian Democrats of Chile, despite anything that the Communists may say to the contrary, do not consider themselves to be the defenders of capitalism. This is very much in accord with current Latin American thinking. Latin Americans today, particularly those of the middle class (many of the workers have in any case for years been opposed to capitalism), resist the idea that the only alternative to Communism is the capitalism of the "free enterprise" variety. This is reflected in many of the social statements made by bishops who condemn the evils of capitalism as well as those of Communism. As Bishop Larraín of Talca told me in Santiago: "We realize that the capitalist era is finished and that, as was noted by Pope John in his encyclical *Mater et Magistra*, we are going into a socialized era. If Communism is unacceptable to us, then we must find an alternative, but it does not have to be capitalism."

This is the attitude of many of Chile's middle class, and it was this that led them to desert the Radical party for the Christian Democrats. Many of the votes which went to Frei from this class reflected not so much support for Christian Democracy as a search for something which belongs neither to Moscow nor to Washington, something which is neither Communist nor capitalist.

Similarly, the Christian Democrats take a stand against any form of totalitarianism. As a matter of deliberate policy they are the first to speak out against the military coups and military juntas which have so often been Latin America's only reply to the threat of Communism. "It is essential that this government should be seen to be no one's puppet," one Church leader told me.

I asked Raúl Troncoso, the minister who is Secretary to the Cabinet, to explain why it was that his government had reacted so quickly and so adversely to the American Marines going into the Dominican Republic. He said that they believed that the way to defeat Communism was not by force and the use of the big stick, but by mutual respect. If this was true within their own country, then they must demonstrate that they believed it also to be the case in foreign affairs.

They place their hopes on being able to build international relations which are based on mutual respect between nations. This explains why the students' and workers' demonstrations which occurred in Santiago at the time of America's intervention in Santo Domingo took the form of a united protest by Christian Democrats, Socialists, and Communists. By this means the violence which the Communists would have provoked was syphoned into a largely peaceful protest—although the Communist press naturally made the most of the relatively few incidents the Communists were able to engineer.

High in the government's priorities is the reform of industry and the labor laws. These latter affect agricultural as well as industrial workers. William Thayer, the Minister of Labor, told me that, with the assistance of the International Labor Office, he was aiming to simplify and make effective the whole of the existing labor legislation. There would be a new law which would create the machinery for collective bargaining for every worker. The need for the modernization of employer-worker relations was already recognized by the majority of industrialists—and this was one reason why they were prepared to support the Christian Democrats with their votes. Very little resistance to the new legislation had, in fact, come from them. The majority of the trade union leaders approved what the government intended to do. The minister told me that he doubted if more than a few thousand farm workers were organized at all. Even so, and this reflects the atmosphere of change which pervades Chile today, he believed that there would be little opposition from the landowners to the "unionization" of their workers.

The minister did not minimize the Communist danger in Chile. He acknowledged its presence and foresaw that the Communists would make a gigantic effort to produce the downfall of the government. But like other Christian Democrat leaders, his was the positive approach. "We believe we'll bring the Communists to their knees," he told me, "if we go forward with our own plans. In a world which is growing more just, Communism will grow weaker, provided that we have our eyes open and understand what they are trying to do."

One of the government's main problems in trying to bring about a social revolution within the framework of parliamentary democracy is clearly likely to be that of the sheer mechanics of getting a vast mass of legislation through parliament at high speed without appearing to steam-roller parliamentary processes.

A great deal obviously turned on its ability to show early results. This required quickly carrying into law the new agrarian reform, the reform of the labor laws, the business reform, family allowances, and a great deal of legislation on education. Frei's greatest problem became how to maintain a climate of opinion favorable to rapid change and the "mystique" of Christian social revolution, both of which were essential if the reforms were quickly to be pushed through.

The government aims to give land to a hundred thousand families, using both expropriation and compensation in its efforts to get the land required. Typically, the land reform offers a choice of either "collectivized" agriculture or individual holdings to the settlers who benefit by it.

Statistics prepared by the U.S. Department of Agriculture in 1962 emphasize just how urgent is the need for sweeping agrarian reform. These show that 62.8 per cent of Chile's farms are under 50 acres and together they occupy only 0.2 per cent of the total farming land. On the other hand, 0.5 per cent of the farms are over 1,235 acres. These occupy 48 per cent of total farming land. It is small wonder that the Frei government puts the job of implementing land reform high on the list of priorities.

In the light of these figures one can see why Chile, like other Latin American countries, suffers from a drift from the land. This in turn has led to the usual growth of huge shanty towns. An ambitious housing program is therefore seen as an essential and urgent part of the government's plan for social reconstruction.

Like Brazil, Chile has for long been plagued with runaway inflation. The ever-rising cost of living for 30 years on end has caused continuous hardship to the public, and from time to time has led to unrest which erupted into violent demonstrations and so played directly into the hands of the Communists. The Frei government's answer to inflation is a positive one. It is to initiate a great public works program, increase government spending on housing and slum clearance, stimulate economic development, and thus insure full employment.

Twelve months after he was given his working majority, President Frei was able to report that ten times as many schools had been built as the annual average for the previous five years, the target of the national housing plan had been exceeded, the infant mortality rate had been reduced, and the rate of inflation had been cut from 50 per cent in 1964 to 25 per cent. There had been a 12 per cent rise in the purchasing power of the poorest workers.

CHRISTIAN TRADE UNIONS

It happens that CLASC (*Confederación Latinoamericana de Sindicalistas Cristianos*), the Latin American Federation of Christian Trade Unions, has its headquarters in Santiago de Chile. Operating from there, its leaders travel from country to country building up the Christian trade unions. They are encouraged from outside by the International Federation of Christian Trade Unions, the worldwide organization headed by Auguste Vanistendaal with headquarters in Belgium.

The current trend in the Catholic Church, particularly since Pope John XXIII, is away from every sort of Catholic "ghetto." Confessional trade unions, like confessional parties, belong more to the Church's defensive, inward-turning period. Today the emphasis is on dialogue, on the Christian going into the secular world. This is reflected within the International Federation of Christian Trade Unions itself, whose affiliates tend now to stress their nonconfessional character, basing themselves on Christian principles rather than on formal links with the Church.

The CLASC leaders in Santiago insist that their affiliated bodies in Latin America are not confessional unions. Some are still at the stage where they are in the hands of the priests who first organized them. Others are completely in the hands of Christian and other laymen. Generally speaking, Christian unions tend today to be more militant than those affiliated to ORIT; they pride themselves on their independence and their greater suitability to Latin American conditions.

Chile's Christian Democrats, even though they had the support of the local CLASC unions in the elections, see no particular reason why they should support only unions with the word Christian in their title. After all, a strong case can be made out for Christians taking their influence into the other unions.

Señor Goldsack, CLASC's president, told me that the Christian unions were having to fight for supremacy on the basis of proven ability to defend the workers' interests, and this was a situation of which he approved. He looked for no favors from the Christian Democrat government.

The question of the rôle of the Christian trade unions, as opposed to the Christian in the non-Christian trade union, is one which is currently being fiercely argued in political and trade union circles in most of the countries of

Latin America. To an outside Christian observer it would appear obvious that in the case of unions which are not completely Communist-controlled there is everything to be said for Christians remaining inside and working to keep them as close as possible to Christian principles.

One of the strongest arguments in support of CLASC unions is that these come nearer to representing the mind and mood of Latin America than any in which either the U.S. or Communist influence is dominant. It is not simply a question of international connections as such. The International Federation of Christian Trade Unions is European-based and has a Belgian as its Secretary-General. In Europe its strength tends to be in France, Belgium, Holland, and Germany. But many Latin Americans have a greater sense of kinship with any or all of these countries than with either the U.S.A. or the U.S.S.R.

There is a Latin American culture. Nonetheless, historically, it is a borrowed one—borrowed from Europe, and still fed from Europe. Current trends in French, German, Dutch, and Belgian Catholic thought, for example, probably count for more in Latin American Christian thinking than anything that comes from elsewhere. From the time of the French Revolution, Latin America has also drawn upon Europe for its political thinking, usually keeping half a generation behind. But these various European streams, cultural, religious, and political, do add up to something which is distinctively Latin American. It is against this background that the Christian trade unions genuinely appear to have something which is more Latin American to offer than have the other unions. They have that "mystique" for which the Latin American looks.

So, like it or not, Christian Democrats and others must

be prepared to see the Christian unions grow in precisely this period when elsewhere the trend is away from unions of this type.

No one is more conscious of the need for social revolution than the CLASC leaders. And no one is doing more to influence public opinion toward the reconstruction of the social order along lines which are neither capitalist nor Communist. This may well be the course which Latin America will take in its political evolution in the years ahead. So the Christian unions, either affiliated to CLASC or maintaining an independent existence, as some do, must be reckoned among the forces making for change in Latin America today.

THE COMMUNISTS

When trying to deal with the Church and Catholics, Communists everywhere traditionally tried to separate the "goodies" from the "badies." In practice this has meant, on the basis of campaigns on urgent issues, attempting to bring the Catholic masses into a united front while simultaneously denouncing Church and Catholic political leaders as reactionaries.

This was the policy which the Communist party of Chile pursued in the past. It was able to maintain it throughout the early period of the rise of the Christian Democrats—which coincided, of course, with the period in which the Church became increasingly outspoken on the social question. But the word *reactionary*, as we have seen, began to look less and less convincing as time went on. No one could justly deny that the Christian Democrat leaders and the Church, as represented by its most prominent spokesmen and the active section of the Catholic laity, were helping along the process of social change.

If the Communist party continued to denounce the ecclesiastical leaders in the old way, it might very well forfeit all hope of winning the Catholic masses to its side. For if they were sufficiently politically alert to be attracted to Communism, they were equally likely to be appreciative of what their bishops were doing. If, on the other hand, to please the Catholic masses, the Communists acknowledged the sincerity of the bishops' intentions, they would cut the ground from under their own feet by making it seem that the Communist revolution had been rendered obsolete by the Christian social revolution.

Again, on foreign issues a similar problem presented itself. It would have been easy had the Christian Democrat leaders talked Left before being elected, then acted Right as soon as they had the responsibility of government. Chile's Christian Democrats did nothing of the sort. Just how do you drive wedges between "reactionary" leaders and "progressive" rank and file when those leaders start talking business with the Eastern European countries as soon as they are elected, work with American capitalists to aid the copper industry, yet jump in more smartly than anyone to condemn U.S. intervention when the Marines, to the delight of Communists all over the rest of Latin America, go into Santo Domingo? In such circumstances, to attack the leaders is likely only to solidify the support of the rank and file behind them.

An anonymous Latin American Communist leader, quoting Luis Corvalán, General Secretary of the Communist party of Chile, wrote in the World Marxist Review of May, 1965, "With regard to the Christian Democratic government the Communist party has adopted an 'attitude of firm and active but not blind opposition' which presupposes 'steady action on behalf of the working people and the masses generally, in defense of the common interests of the nation, democratic rights, and social gains'." According to Corvalán's analysis, Eduardo Frei personifies the "reformist bourgeoisie" and "dreads the mass movement, without which no far-reaching reforms are possible."

The Latin American revolution has been described as a "revolution of rising expectations." The people of Chile expect much of the Frei government. And they expect it to come quickly. It is undoubtedly the government's intention to give them just as much as possible as quickly as possible. But there are limits to what can be done immediately.

Before land reform can be made something more than a scrap of paper, a great deal of information has to be gathered and collated; the lawyers must prepare the title deeds before the government's representatives start handing out the land. The beneficial consequences of new labor laws are not necessarily felt in the first few months. The Russians long ago discovered that, even if one bulldozes down the slums, it still takes time to rehouse people. Moreover, under Latin American conditions, while one is pulling down one slum and rehousing its population, new thousands are pouring in from the countryside, creating new and bigger ones. It may not be difficult to persuade those for whom the reforms are intended that they were given promises, but have been denied the realities.

If the government continues to steal the Communists' thunder by pressing quickly ahead with its reforms, the Communists may turn "selective obstruction" to economic and industrial sabotage in the form of waves of strikes in decisive industries. But alternatively this may take the form of sabotage of the other sort.

The Communist party of Chile is one of the oldest and most experienced in Latin America. Its formal existence as a Communist party, affiliated to the Comintern, began in 1921, although, in fact, it started its life as the Socialist Workers' party of Chile as long ago as 1912. During the course of its life it has had experience both of the "constitutional struggle" during periods of legality and of the "underground struggle" during long periods of illegality. Luis Corvalán has declared that the party still does not rule out force as a means of coming to power.

The party does not publish its membership figures, but in 1965 they were estimated, by those who should know, at something between 20,000 and 25,000, with a voting strength of 300,000. The party has one daily and one weekly paper. Since the daily is said to have a circulation of not much more than 5,000, this would suggest that the party's hard core is much smaller than its total membership. Even so, it is still capable of generating a good deal of mischief.

The Christian Democrats are very conscious that the world is watching what they do and that the course of Christian Democracy, and of social revolution, in Latin America may be determined by their success or failure. This is recognized and acknowledged by the Communists too. The *World Marxist Review* has described the "special rôle" of "the Frei party" as being to demonstrate by its success "the attractiveness of the Christian Democratic alternative for all the countries of Latin America."

Almost certainly a battle lies ahead in Chile. It is a battle between the best that Latin America has got in both camps. But at this stage of the struggle the initiative is with the Christian Democrats; it is they who look most like "the wave of the future."

For years Latin American Communists thrived on the popular belief that it was they who were Latin America's most dynamic group, the irresistible force, the wave of the future. They also gained from the fact that this drove the land-owning class, the military caste, and also many of the new "bourgeoisie," into frightened support for military juntas or demagogues who ranged from benevolent authoritarians to blood-thirsty dictators of the type of Batista in Cuba and Pérez Jiménez in Venezuela.

The Church and the Christian Democrats of Chile have between them demonstrated that there is, to put it at its lowest, a counter-dynamic which challenges Communism on its own ground. One does not now have to be a Communist to demand and work for the total transformation of the social structure of his country. Chile has demonstrated that this can be done within the framework of democracy and, if one is a Christian, within the Church itself.

Moreover, in the process, Chile's Christian Democrats have destroyed the myth that the Cuban pattern is the only one for a Latin America in travail.

Taking the Other Road

8

Financiers and businessmen were jumping out of windows in Rio de Janeiro and São Paulo in mid-1965, on a scale probably not seen anywhere since the great Wall Street crash of 1929.

The number of Brazil's unemployed was soaring week by week. So were prices, as they had been doing for years. Work in one factory after another slowed down, then stopped altogether. Hardly a car or refrigerator had been sold for months. Agents were being told that they could slash their prices as they pleased, just so that some cash would at least be coming in with which to go on paying the remaining workers.

I had flown into Rio straight from Santiago de Chile. There could have been no greater contrast between the policies of two countries at that moment. Both had for years been faced with runaway inflation. Influential sections of the public in each believed that their country had come close to the very brink of Communism. For myself, I would say that this was more true of Chile than of Brazil, although in neither was the threat immediate and direct.

The Marxist Popular Action Front of Communists and Socialists could have won the elections in Chile and, had it done so, the Communist party was sufficiently well-led for it to be possible that it might before long have got the reins effectively into its own hands. Had the military not swept aside President João Goulart's government in the 1964 coup and put Humberto Castelo Branco[1] in power, Brazil might possibly have sunk into economic and political anarchy, but it is extremely doubtful that this would have led to a Communist Brazil—if only because the country's Communist party was too weak and divided to exploit such a situation.

By the time Artur da Costa e Silva succeeded Castelo Branco in March, 1967, a pattern of predominantly military rule had been set which was in sharp contrast to the rule of the Frei government in Chile. It has been described as "authoritarian presidentialism and centralism."

In its three years of rule the Castelo Branco government pursued a deflationary policy and was able to report that the country's rate of inflation was 41.1 per cent in 1966 as compared with the 85 per cent in the last year of the Goulart government. This no doubt justified it in the eyes of the economists, though not in those of the Brazilian poor. Castelo Branco's policies eased some economic and administrative problems. But his government brought about no social change, still less any change in the social structure. Social problems remained as acute as ever.

Chile and Brazil, these two neighboring countries, provide some fascinating contrasts. The response to the Communist threat, real or imagined, on the part of the governments of Eduardo Frei and Castelo Branco could hardly

[1] *Killed in an air-crash, July 18, 1967.*

have been more different. Once the Christian Democrats had come to power in Chile, practically no one in authority mentioned the word *Communism*. They did not blind themselves to its existence; they were just getting on with the job of trying to end the conditions out of which Communism grows. In Castelo Branco's Brazil, hardly anyone in authority talked of anything but Communism. Brazil, said the rich, had but recently been saved from the fate of Castro's Cuba, though how that could be so when the Goulart regime had crumbled in 48 hours, it was hard to see. There were, allegedly, Communists everywhere. No one at the top drew any distinction between democratic socialism and Communism, and most drew none between liberalism and Communism either.

Catholic lay organizations whose dedicated activists were selflessly working among the poorest of the poor were condemned as Communist; bishops and archbishops who had spoken out on the social question were smeared with the Communist brush; one or two priests and more laymen had been clapped into prison as subversives.

The Frei government's response to the inflationary situation it had inherited was to boost the economy by means of ambitious and urgently needed public works programs. The Castelo Branco government's response to inflation was to run the economy down, cutting right back on all public spending.

The Frei government had been the first to condemn the U.S. intervention in Santo Domingo. The Castelo Branco government had been the first to offer to send in its troops to fight shoulder to shoulder with the Marines.

The Frei government was determined to be nobody's stooge. It was prepared to receive assistance and advice from qualified people in half a dozen European countries and, if need be, from Americans who were genuinely willing to help, but it was absolutely convinced of the necessity of maintaining independence. The Castelo Branco government made no secret of its dependence upon the U.S.A. The economic policy which it was pursuing was that recommended by American advisers. Behind much of its thinking appeared to be the idea that the stability of the entire hemisphere might be made to depend upon a U.S.A.-Brazilian alliance.

Around the Frei government were intellectuals whose views were respected—reminiscent of John F. Kennedy days in Washington, D.C. Intellectuals in the Brazil of Castelo Branco were suspect—victims of an attitude toward "eggheads" more reminiscent of the days of Senator McCarthy in the U.S.

The Frei government knew that its hopes were bound up with its ability to gain the support of the working people, and it was determined to create in them a sense of involvement in the revolution it was trying to launch. The Castelo Branco government called its coup a "revolution," but it was openly seeking to solve the problems of the existing system by a deflationary policy which involved increasing the number of unemployed, lowering the standards of the poorest of the poor, and setting itself against what had been the growing involvement of the people in the solution of their own problems. Eduardo Frei and his government were nothing if not democratic. Castelo Branco's government was unashamedly authoritarian.

Yet Eduardo Frei and Castelo Branco were both practicing Catholics; each claimed to want a more Christian society. Here, on the face of it, was indeed a confrontation between the new and the old. I have deliberately drawn the contrasts in somewhat stark and over-simplified terms, but it is the way many Latin Americans see them. For this reason, it is true to say that, if Frei succeeds, the new Christian Democracy will have been helped all over Latin America, and the effectiveness of a new and more positive approach to the Communist threat will have been established. If Marshal Costa e Silva succeeds and Frei fails, the case of social reform will have been put back, and every old-type Latin American conservative who has always believed that the solution to every political problem is to restrict democratic rights and to bring in the military as soon as things go wrong, will be saying, "I told you so."

The very real difference between the personal positions of the two presidents gives some inkling of the difference in the two situations. Frei is surrounded by men who share his mind, follow his lead. His policies are carried into effect by people who share his political philosophy, accept his aims and methods. Castelo Branco was ever under pressure from "wild men" of the Right who distrusted him and who were directly responsible for some of his government's more repressive measures. They prided themselves on their authoritarian toughness, distrusted what they regarded as his all-too-democratic softness.

The success of Chile's Christian Democrats at the polls in 1964 and 1965 represented the culmination of years of preparation and organization. It was a result of the activities of a growing mass movement, the product of a new climate of opinion. Castelo Branco's coming to power was the result of a military revolt by a small group of men who, seeing their country drifting into chaos, decided that enough is enough. A positive program brought Frei to power; a largely negative attempt to end an ever-worsening economic and political situation gave Castelo Branco the presidency, and it was this that his successors inherited.

To further underline the complexity of the two situations: each government had the support of its local Christian trade union movement—but the leaders of the two movements were not on speaking terms because each was convinced that the other was utterly wrong. Each government had the support of people who called themselves Christian Democrats. But those who supported Frei were authentically democratic and represented something entirely new in Latin American life, while those who supported Castelo Branco typified the Catholic conservatives who over the years have supported every reactionary regime throughout Central and South America.

SIZE OF THE PROBLEM

Brazil is not a country; it is an empire. Or, rather, it was before it became a republic. Latin America was divided between Portugal and Spain. The Portuguese called their half of the subcontinent Brazil.

It is bigger than the U.S.A. without Alaska. It has more than ten times the area of Chile and some nine and a half times its population. Brazil's population growth creates very real problems; but if its vast resources were utilized, it would have no problem, for huge areas remain totally undeveloped. One gets a more accurate picture of Brazil if one thinks of it, not as a single country, but as a number of different countries at very differing stages of development, ranging from highly sophisticated Rio de Janeiro and São

Paulo, to the wildest of jungle country inhabited by the most primitive of Indians.

Brazilians are conscious of the fact that, given time, or outside assistance, or both, they have all the human and material resources required to become one of the world's leading nations. The building of the new capital of Brasilia by President Kubitschek was an expression of this self-confidence and of the enormous thrust and energy which are characteristic of the middle class of the southern cities today. But it made the problem of inflation, already severe, even worse.

Along with chronic economic instability has gone political instability, aftermath of a corporate state which was modeled on that of Mussolini and Salazar. It seemed that a new era was dawning when Jânio Quadros was elected in 1961, but he had not the support of Congress, and he dashed the hopes of those who put their faith in him when he suddenly resigned. He was replaced by João Goulart; this caused as much consternation to the Right as if U.S. Vice-President Henry Wallace had been obliged suddenly to take over from President Franklin D. Roosevelt.

Mercifully for Brazil, the Communist party was bitterly divided. Its founders had become the "elder statesmen" of the party. They had lost effective control of it, and no one of the same calibre had arisen to take their places. However, by dubbing everyone left of center a Communist, their opponents were able to create the impression both within Brazil and abroad that this huge country was about to drop into the Communists' lap; and in April, 1964, the army, with the blessing of the United States, overthrew Goulart's government and installed Marshal Humberto Castelo Branco in his place. Brazil had returned to authoritarian

Modern farming methods in Chile.

A Chilean adult realizing his dream to read and write.

Jungle travel along the Amazon in Brazil.

A Brazilian housewife outside her barracks-like shack in Rio de Janeiro. In background is an ultra-modern church.

Logs in a lumberyard await cutting display one of Brazil's greatest natural resources.

A Brazilian peasant, suffering from hunger and malnutrition, in the vast, parched, undeveloped land upon which he is dependent for his life.

A slum area resident in Rio de Janeiro carries cans to a well
to obtain water for his shack.

Negro workers in a field in north-east Brazil.

rule with none of her political or pressing economic problems solved.

Opinions about Marshal Castelo Branco conflict wildly. Roughly, one may say, priests and laymen who have worked with the very poor tend to regard his "revolution" as a disaster. This, however, needs to be qualified because he had the support of some of the Christian trade unions who admittedly go back in their origins to the period of the corporate State. Moreover, although his government was strongly anti-Communist, this does not mean it showed no concern for social justice. For example, its land reform, had it been carried into effect, would possibly have been better than anything attempted by the previous government. But to almost anyone who is left of center in Brazilian politics, the Castelo Branco regime represented a return to the country's near-Fascist past.

Most people right of center, including Catholic conservatives, of whom there are many in the middle and upper classes, believe that the Castelo Branco government saved their country from Communism, and the Church from possible extinction.

Foreign observers in Brazil, who can perhaps more easily stand aside from recent events, tend to take the view that, imperfect as the regime was, it was probably the best available in the circumstances. Marshal Castelo Branco is generally credited with having been an honest authoritarian. Had he been a power-hungry dictator, he would not have moved from the center of the political scene when he considered that his particular job had been completed.

His government contained some genuinely Christian leaders and a few who had some concern for democracy. But it also included some political wild men who, whatever their religion might or might not be, were prepared to use thoroughly un-Christian methods against their opponents. Again, to keep the picture as straight as one can, it needs to be noted that, while repressive measures were taken at government level and while there were excesses here and there at the local level, the worst excesses of the early days of Dictator Vargas, for example, were avoided.

That the issues cannot just be presented in terms of black and white is strikingly illustrated by the fact that a prospective British Parliamentary Labor candidate could write in a booklet[1] published by the socialist Fabian Society as follows:

"What, constitutionally, can be done under a Presidential system when governmental action is urgent but impossible? Under a Parliamentary system the answer is simple. One changes the Government and, if necessary, re-elects the Parliament. But under a Presidential system there is no answer unless the President is prepared to resign. If he is not, there is deadlock and a complete breakdown in the governmental machine. Constitutionally, therefore, Brazil had reached an *impasse* from which there was no constitutional exit.

"Under this type of circumstance, which can easily arise in an under-developed country operating according to the American type of Presidential system, one of the functions of the military is to bend the constitution from time to time so that effective government can be carried on. It should not be made into a tragedy that this type of intervention has once more been necessary in Brazil. It is no doubt regrettable. But anyone weeping over Goulart is wasting his tears. Reform is no less likely today than it was un-

[1] *Brazil: The Dilemma of Reform.* By Edmund Dell. London, 1964.

der Goulart. It may be more. A more conservative government may, in fact, provide a better opportunity for enacting those reforms for which a consensus has been established than a more radical government whose further intentions are mistrusted."

Alfredo Castro, writing in the August, 1966, issue of the *World Marxist Review*, made some interesting admissions of mistakes made by the Communists. "We slipped down more and more to extremist positions," he wrote, "until finally the reactionaries, the agents of imperialism, taking advantage of our blunders, became the standard-bearers of democratic legality." By then, he went on, broad sections of the national and urban petty bourgeoisie had "turned to the camp of reaction," so that, when the coup took place, the radicals were already isolated.

It may be argued that the Castelo Branco government made the job of Communists throughout Latin America easier by helping to undermine the case against Communism. It is inevitable that in developing countries many people will be attracted by the promise of rapid development under Communism. They hardly dare dream of ever being able to achieve, certainly not in the foreseeable future, the material prosperity of the U.S.A. But that of the Communist countries would seem an attainable aim. One of the few telling arguments against this is that the price they would have to pay in the loss of civil liberties and of the rights of the individual is too high for what they get in return in the way of material things. The Castelo Branco government dealt toughly with people of the Left, ranging from progressive Catholics to Communists—and often failed to distinguish the two in any case. When it took repressive measures against political opponents and those

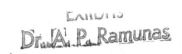

trade unionists whom it did not like, it was guilty of exactly what the Communists are charged with doing.

The new constitution, which Marshal Costa e Silva's government inherited from it, confirmed the military in their positions, gave wide powers to military courts, and limited the democratic liberties of citizens.

This is an all-too-familiar Latin American tradition, and even though the repressions in the Brazil of today may be mild by comparison with some that Latin America has known in the past, the confirmation of military and authoritarian rule in a new constitution tends to perpetuate that tradition which for years has played into the Communists' hands. Even the worst excesses in Soviet jails during the years of Stalin's rule have their parallel in what occurred in Latin American prisons during the rule of dictators like Batista of Cuba and Pérez Jiménez of Venezuela. What, perhaps more than anything, Latin America requires today is a break with all that and a genuine attempt at achieving social revolution by democratic means. No such lead as that can be hoped for under Brazil's new constitution.

It was from a priest in Rio that I learned of the rosary's being put to what would seem to many to be a somewhat bizarre use. A rosary crusade was organized in São Paulo just when feeling was building up in conservative circles against President Goulart and his inefficient government, and when his opponents were most loudly denouncing his regime as Communist. As is usual with "crusades" of this type, one of its aims was to implore the Blessed Virgin to save the country from Communism. The idea had a particular point and purpose for the well-to-do women of the city who were already convinced that, short of a supernatural intervention, the country was likely to go Communist at any moment.

The crusade built up into mass demonstrations of women reciting the rosary with the intention that Brazil be preserved from the fate of Cuba. Whatever the supernatural effect of this may or may not have been, it certainly had a profound human and, indeed, political effect. President Goulart complained not unnaturally that all this was being directed against him and his government. Many of the women who led the great rosary processions still claim, possibly with some justification, that they were the means by which Goulart was brought down and Castelo Branco brought to power.

It is not unreasonable to suggest that the crusade did in fact convince the men who led the military coup that they would have the support of important sections of the public for any action they might take against Goulart and his followers. Foreign political commentators with no particular feeling for rosary crusades have gone on record with the opinion that the processions touched off the "revolution." The rosary had been made an effective political weapon.

The religious demonstrations also had the side effect of convincing many of the people in the slums that the Church was identified with a coup which they believed was aimed at saving the privileges of the wealthy at the expense of the well-being of the impoverished masses.

The priest to whom I talked was particularly concerned by the adverse effect of all this upon intellectuals whose alienation from the Church had been made more complete. But, he reasoned, if the rosary had been used as a weapon once—and some might think for rather dubious purposes—

why should it not be used again, this time for a good purpose? So he had drawn up a document in which he equated
the various mysteries of the rosary with different aspects
of the fight for social justice. He was somewhat optimisti-
cally hoping that on the basis of this it might be possible to
work up another great rosary crusade, this time to implore
Mary to lead members of the Castelo Branco government
along the path of social justice, inspire the rich to concern
themselves with the sufferings of the poor, and prompt the
poor to work for their own social betterment. Even if his
crusade ever got off the ground, its aim, I fear, would be a
good deal more difficult to achieve than that of bringing
down Goulart's ramshackle government. And it would require a minor miracle to be able to even begin to awaken
the same enthusiasm among most of São Paulo's wealthy
women for this very different set of intentions.

CATHOLIC SOCIAL MOVEMENT

It would be quite wrong to suppose that Brazil's ecclesiastical leaders and the Catholic laity are solidly on the side
of the forces of reaction. On the contrary, some of Brazil's
200 bishops are as progressive as any. And its "wooden
cross" bishops are known to Christians the world over for
their break with traditional pomp and their attempt to return to the simplicity of the early Christians.

As is to be expected, a high proportion of these are to
be found among the 50 bishops of the Northeast, practically every one of whom functions against a background of
poverty, hunger, and illiteracy.

It is hardly surprising, either, that some of the country's
most vigorous Christian social movements flourish among

the 30 million people of that area. If there were no Catholics prepared to take exceptional measures in an attempt to lift up the poor of the Northeast from the sub-human conditions in which they live, then the outside world would, indeed, be justified in believing that Brazil's social conscience was dead.

It was to the great sugar plantations of the Northeast that the slaves were brought by the thousands centuries ago. They came in ships bearing names of saints, to ports with names like São Salvador, and from there spread out over the huge Portuguese empire. But the largest concentration remained in the area to which they were first brought.

For this reason there are more Negroes and mulattoes there than elsewhere in Brazil. And whereas in other parts they have been absorbed into the larger community, in the Northeast, because of their sheer numbers, they still tend to live as separate communities. Not only are they concentrated, for example, in the areas where their slave ancestors toiled among the sugar, but they may still be found on the same plantations, even living in the same houses.

Brazil prides itself on being free of race and color consciousness. This may be so. It is also true that the Negroes of the Northeast remain a sub-group. In a land which, at the higher social levels at least, has a culture of European origin, the conditions in which vast millions of the population live are much closer to those of India than of Europe.

Along the waterfront of Penang Island, in the South China Sea, one may see the wooden homes of several hundred squatters who have built their shacks on stilts out over the water's edge. In Salvador, in the Brazilian State of Bahia, there are thousands of such homes. But they are smaller, more decayed, more precariously perched above the water and very much less easily accessible to those who live in them.

It had been raining the day I visited the waterside slums, and the unmade-up roads which led to them were rivers of mud. The slums came up to the water's edge, then spilled out over the water itself. Presumably the first-comers had chosen the site because the river would provide drinking water, washing water, and a ready-made sewer. The later arrivals had no place to go except over the water itself. So they built their diminutive wooden shacks on stilts reached by means of narrow planks. Then more came whose shacks were erected still further out. Today one can wander for hundreds of yards over the inadequate and dangerous "bridges" which lead on from one rotting dilapidated shack to the next.

Yet the Negroes and mulattoes who live in these degrading conditions have a great and natural pride. They carry themselves with the easy grace of the African. From dwellings which would be condemned as dog kennels elsewhere, one may see Negro women in clean, carefully pressed, and gaily colored dresses emerging to walk, with straight back and head held high, along the rotting planks. Heaven alone knows how many meals are sacrificed to buy those dresses. But it is by such means that somehow, almost miraculously, they retain their dignity. They may live in sub-human conditions, but so long as they can hold out, they scrape and save and sacrifice to dress themselves decently, determined not to descend to the level of those who live in rags.

Visitors to these slums, like the rich ladies of Rio slumming in the *favelas* of the southern cities, are often shocked by the way in which the poor will sacrifice food to keep up appearances. To them it seems to reflect a false sense of values. But I wonder? The evidence seems to suggest that when people in these conditions cease to care about appearances they take the last step on the way to total human degradation.

Most such areas, and this is true throughout Latin America, have one feast day of the year on which, to the outside observer, the people go mad. They save for it for months. Money which, according to any nutritional expert, ought to be spent on food is spent on clothes—and, certainly so far as the men are concerned, on alcohol too. It is easy to say, as many do, that this is sheer stupidity. Yet if the sum spent was spread over the year they would still be living in degrading slums, and far below the poverty line. And 365 days of the year would be gray. As it is, for one or two out of the 365, life becomes gay, the drabness and squalor of life in the slums is forgotten. For 24 hours they are the kings and queens of the earth.

In terms of cold common sense it may be hard to justify the money spent. The material loss is obvious. But it may well be that what they gain is an ability somehow, despite everything that society has done against them, to remain human.

The same may be said concerning the television aerials (not all of which have television sets attached) which may be seen rising above some of the worst slums of Latin America. Concern with status symbols may be a disquieting feature of suburban life in more affluent lands. A status symbol in the slums of Latin America may be a sign of one man's desperate attempt to retain a hold on his dignity as a human being.

And so it is, too, with those Negro women wearing their newly washed, gaily colored frocks in the waterfront slums of Salvador, Bahia. They may live in a stinking quagmire, but they can still hold their heads high.

It was evening when I was taken to a Negro quarter on the city's outskirts. In the darkness we groped our way along narrow unmade roads to the *Capoeira* "Academy." In a room in a private dwelling two Negroes and a tall, tough-looking, "poor white" sat on a bench playing tambourines with enormous intensity. Two more Negroes were playing *berimbaus*.

The *berimbau* looks like a gaily painted longbow made of bamboo with just one wire string. Attached to the bow is a large, brightly painted coconut shell with an open end. The bow is held with the left hand and jerked rhythmically up and down. With each upward jerk, the open end of the coconut is thrust on to the bare and sweating chest of the player who thus produces a sucking sound. In his other hand he holds a long, pointed plectrum. Attached to this is a gaily colored rattle which emits its own sound as the plectrum is used to pluck the string. Thus a single player produces at one and the same time the sounds of plucking, sucking, and rattling.

The *berimbau* players, like the tambourine players, were putting everything they had into their music. Sweat ran down their faces and bodies; their open shirts were already saturated. As they played, they also sang. The rhythm of the sung music was different from that of the music they played. The words were repeated many times over. Sometimes these were simply the name of God and various saints in Portuguese. Sometimes, they were in some dimly remembered African language, said to be a corrupted form of a tribal language from Angola—an echo of the days before the Negroes' ancestors had been brought here as slaves. When this language was used, the singers called on African pagan gods to come to their aid, or harked back to slave-trading days in the African bush. It was a strange experience to hear descendants of slaves singing, for example, over and over again as they worked themselves into a frenzy, the words "get that nigger, get that nigger."

With equal vigor and intensity, two Negro dancers conducted with great skill a mock "fight" which appeared to come nearer to Japanese judo than to Western wrestling but with this difference: although, crouched low, they circled endlessly around, going through the motions of gripping, striking, kicking, and throwing their partners, neither touched the other at any point. When one maneuvered the other into a position where he could throw him if he wished, he would mime the act of throwing, and his "opponent" would simulate being thrown and land with a thud on the floor. Endlessly, to the accompaniment of the music produced by the sweating instrumentalists, they circled around, crashing from time to time on the boards. They stood on their heads, turned somersaults, did cartwheels, stood on their hands, all at great speed and still were able, following set rules scrupulously observed, to maintain the grace and precision of ballet dancers.

"For power, strength, and energy," said the notice in Portuguese hanging on the wall. The dancers needed all these and a considerable grace and sense of rhythm besides. Capoeira is, in fact, much more than a dance; it is a cult. It is, it would seem, largely a throwback to voodoo and the pagan rites of Africa from which the slaves were brought centuries ago.

Archbishop Eugenio Sales, Apostolic Administrator in Salvador, on one occasion put into words what many of the bishops of the Northeast feel. "Before, we tried to fight for social justice by asking money from the rich and giving charity to the poor. Now we see that we must fight by changing the social structure itself. When the structure is unjust, it should be modified."

"Dom Eugenio," as he is known to everyone, was away from home during the period of my visit; he had gone up to Natal where until a year or two ago he held a similar ecclesiastical position. The names of Dom Eugenio and Natal are still linked because of the "Natal Movement" with which he was and continues to be associated. This was one of the most ambitious pastoral and social-betterment efforts ever undertaken by the Church in Brazil.

In Dom Eugenio's absence, I saw his Auxiliary, Bishop d'Adriano M. Hypolito, O.F.M., at the minor seminary for poor boys at which he lives. The bishop was dressed in his Franciscan habit and sandals. He wore neither pectoral cross, nor ring, nor any other visible evidence of his rank. What Dom Eugenio had done in Natal would be done also in Salvador, he told me. But whereas Natal had 120,000 people, Salvador has 800,000, and therefore they would have to aim at the same thing, but on a bigger scale. When Dom Eugenio was himself an auxiliary bishop in Natal, he set about giving a Christian thrust to an ambitious, imaginative, state-sponsored rural aid scheme. The scheme aimed at providing answers to the people's urgent material needs. Dom Eugenio's object was to ensure that to this was linked concern for their human and spiritual needs as well.

There were some, though not many, Communists in the area, and these, as one would expect, tried to get into the new rural syndicates and the Church-sponsored adult education schemes, and to capture the movement generally. But even though they succeeded in capturing a syndicate here and there, they lacked a mass following among the rural poor who have little sympathy for Communism. Dom Eugenio and the priests who worked with him were able without much difficulty to provide a Christian lead.

Bishop d'Adriano M. Hypolito told me that he believed that only religion stood between the poor of the Northeast and Communism. Their feeling for religion was strong, even though their knowledge of it was weak. If the lack of understanding of the fullness of religion was to be corrected, then many more priests were urgently needed. Given better understanding, there would soon be more lay leaders too. Shortage of priests and lay leaders was at the very root of many of the Church's problems. "Here," the bishop said, "we have 100 priests for 1,400,000 people. In the seminary there are only six students so, assuming that they all persevere with their vocations, at the most we will have only six new local priests during the next seven years."

The vocation shortage, he explained, was partly the result of poverty and illiteracy. Thus one could not dissociate the social question from the pastoral one. A change in the country's social structure was urgent. He believed that people would accept change if it had the backing and blessing of the Church, for the rural people, in particular, looked to the Church for guidance in everything. And the Church in the Northeast was today identified in the minds of the people with the attempt to modernize and develop society along human lines.

Change in the social structure was not the task of the Church as such. What the Church could do was to give the people the impulse to change that structure. And this impulse could come by bishops and priests asserting the Church's teachings and principles on the social question, then leaving it to the lay people to apply them in practical fashion. With very few exceptions, the bishops of the Northeast had a great desire to see the big social projects which had been started in the area carried through to their completion.

THE BASIC EDUCATION MOVEMENT

From a conference held in 1958 was established an organization for assisting and supporting the many existing Catholic radio schools which had been inspired by the Colombian experiment. From this emerged Brazil's MEB— *Movimento de Educação de Base* (Basic Education Movement) which has become the most significant and successful movement of its kind. By 1961 MEB had launched a scheme for education "in-depth" of adult illiterates which had been accepted by the President of the Republic and had concluded agreements with the Ministers of Education, Health, Agriculture, and other organizations.

As Marina Bandeira, its moving spirit, explains, although there are bishops on its board of directors, the work of MEB, including administration, finance, and field work, is the responsibility of lay people. Its busy headquarters are in Rio, but most of its work is done on the spot at state and local levels. Since one of the aims of MEB is to develop leaders in a land where, because of its peculiar social and political past, few leaders arise, everything possible is done to use local people at every level of the organization.

At the center there is the National Team which includes teachers, anthropologists, sociologists, psychologists, philosophers, economists, and experts in audio-visual techniques. Members of this team travel the country organizing new state and local teams and supervising the work. Scattered around those places where MEB functions are some 25 radio stations directly operated by MEB—all told, Brazil has some 80 Catholic radio stations. A radio school system is established throughout the area reached by the radio station. Preparatory work includes a detailed study of local problems, discussions with local leaders and authorities, a publicity campaign, and the selection of people who will insure that, when lessons are put over the air, they will reach those for whom they are intended.

Then comes the training of "monitors." The monitor is a member of a local community who is willing to put himself at the service of others with no hope of financial reward. He is the link between the teacher, who puts the lessons out over the radio, and the pupils. Even though the monitor can, as is often the case, only just read and write, he must have qualities of leadership and a sense of responsibility. He will enroll the pupils, bring his class together, write on the blackboard in response to the voice over the radio, encourage pupils to go to the blackboard too, and correct their exercises.

The "school" in which he operates may be a parish hall, a private house, or any other shelter which is available. Lest the term "private house" conjure up pictures of a gathering of the poor in the drawing room of some socially-minded wealthy family, it is perhaps necessary to note that most often it takes the form of a mud-floored, single-roomed hut, home of the monitor himself. Few rural areas where MEB operates have any electricity. But with a roof over his pupils' heads, a little transistor radio, a supply of elementary textbooks, a blackboard, some chalk, and a kerosene lamp the trained monitor goes into action.

MEB is a notable advance on *Escuelas Radiofónicas.* The Colombian organization prepared the way. MEB represents the next big step forward in the use of radio to bring education to Latin America. Its national leaders aim at something more than what they call "alphabetization." They believe that to teach people simply to read and write, in, for example, the conditions found in Brazil's Northeast may lead only to frustration. For unless social development goes hand in hand with education, there will be no outlet for that education. Hopes will be raised only to be dashed again.

At the end of an elementary eight month course, the pupil is normally able to read short texts, write a simple composition, add, subtract, multiply, and divide. But, in addition, the organizers aim that he should be (most often for the first time in his life) awakened to his rôle as a man, capable of accepting responsibility and acting like a responsible person within society. In the Northeast, in particular, centuries of a slave system under which whole communities depended upon the leadership of paternalistic (or not so paternalistic) slave owners have left the majority of people even to this day with no consciousness of their rôle as men. They have no sense of responsibility, no thought that they might be able to make decisions for themselves.

Each daily lesson lasts about an hour. There are a variety of different lessons for different grades. The elementary one teaches those who are coming for education for the first time how to read and write, elementary arithmetic, the rudiments of nutrition, health, personal hygiene, how to live as a member of a family and of the community, the various types of association such as peasant syndicates, trade unions, working men's clubs, mothers' clubs, cooperatives. The course in addition aims at the pupils' spiritual development. Having awakened them to an awareness of the existence of their personal and social problems, it then aims to make them seek solutions and themselves assume responsibility for the raising of their own standard of life and that of their community by means of organization.

Within three years of MEB's obtaining government and ecclesiastical blessing it had nearly 500 people working full time in its national, State, and local teams, nearly 7,500 radio schools providing basic education to nearly 200,000 people. And all this was being done at an average cost of ten U.S. dollars per year for each pupil.

Many pupils have become monitors; others have become leaders of local peasant and labor unions. But practically all who have had the MEB course have been brought to see the need to evolve new ways of thinking, new forms of action. For this reason, the more nervous or conservative of the bishops, even some of those of the Northeast, go so far with MEB, but no farther. They use its ideas and methods for "alphabetization," but, rejecting its textbooks and using their own, do not carry their courses through to what MEB conceives to be the practical application of the Christian message to Brazil's community life and social conditions. Where MEB's courses are followed in their entirety, something much more profound than the educating of illiterates occurs. A ferment of ideas and a movement which expresses itself in a variety of different forms of organization comes into existence. There is a renewal of community life and of the spiritual life of many of those who are educated by them.

As one would expect, the Northeast, with its urgent problems, has attracted MEB's special attention. And, incidentally, MEB in the Northeast attracted the special attention of some of the more ignorant of Army commanders at the time of the 1964 military coup. Here and there its little local offices were raided, its textbooks seized and banned. But nationally MEB continued to be recognized by the new military government and to receive financial assistance from it. It also continued to have the blessing of the majority of bishops. Of all the lay organizations working for change in Brazil, MEB probably has the greatest potentialities for providing help in depth for those sections of society who stand to gain most by change.

Behind the city of Recife, in Pernambuco State, lie the great sugar plantations. A few of these are relatively modern and efficient. Many have hardly changed since the days of slavery. Some still use mules to turn machinery. A trip from the city into the sugar belt takes one straight from the modern world to the world of slave days.

I stopped one day to talk to a Negro woman and her little daughter who were hoeing weeds on the edge of a plantation. The large, bare-footed, sweating woman was doggedly wielding a heavy hoe; the small girl was clearing the uprooted weeds from around the cane.

For a three-day week, and for their combined efforts, they received $1.75. Had they been paid the minimum wage established by law, they would have received that much for a day's work. But, like everyone else, they were on short time and so in no position to argue. The woman accepted the situation fatalistically. Times were bad. The question was, "Would even the present three-day week hold, or would all work come to a stop?"

In Rio I had been told that it was official policy, as recommended by U.S. advisers, that the economy should be "run down," "deflated," "disinflated"—there was a variety of different names for this method of combating the chronic inflation which for so long has been the curse of Brazil. Here one saw the policy at the cutting end, at the level of human lives. The woman seemed almost fearful to stop work long enough to exchange half a dozen sentences with me, wiping the sweat from her eyes as she did so, lest she might lose the few cents she was trying to earn. Even on full-time she would still only get enough for the barest minimum existence. To the economists and financial advisers, had they to endure it themselves, it would be near-starvation.

Farther along the road we stopped at another sugar plantation. This, too, was feeling the effects of disinflation. To get to the refinery, we had first to penetrate the confines of the plantation itself. We might have been entering a concentration camp. Locked gates blocked the private road off from the public highway. These first gates were unlocked for us, and along the road we came to a group of little villas. On their verandahs Mestizo women sat talking to each other. Their menfolk puttered nearby. Close at hand stood the refinery and distillery, silent and motionless. Both were closed.

A single white man, with two or three Negroes assisting

him, was loading bits of machinery on to a truck. Distillery, refinery, and office workers, he told me, had all been laid off. There were no orders. The families living in the little villas I had seen along the road were those of administrative workers. They were unemployed, but, for the moment at least, had enough behind them to be able to get by.

Then, after more unlocking of gates, we went through a high chain-link fence and into the wired-off area where lived workers employed in the refinery and distillery. Their homes were a row of stone huts, each identical to its neighbor, all absolutely minimal, like the most old-fashioned and dilapidated of the Indian "lines" on run-down rubber plantations in Malaya. A high wall had been built at the near-end of the line to shut them off from the neat little "staff" villas on the other side of the fence.

Then through yet another locked gate to the plantation workers' homes on the edge of the sugar fields: these were minute, primitive hovels. They provided some sort of shelter from sun and rain, no more.

My companions were members of a MEB team in Recife who in the past had set up a school in a plantation workers' village on the other side of the vast estate. As we bumped and swayed along the mud road through the tall sugar cane, we caught up with a line of men coming away from their weeding. They carried hoes on their shoulders and were still steaming from their exertions.

All Negroes, they wore ragged shirts, old trousers, and large, battered straw sunhats. Exhausted by their labors, they made their way toward the village silently, each man walking on his own.

One who held his hoe on his shoulder with one hand and carried an umbrella in the other called to us as we passed. The MEB team immediately recognized him as Pedro, monitor of the local radio school. He climbed into our truck, and we drove him to his home in the old slave village. At its center was a small white church outside which stood a figureless cross. This was the slave church. At the cross the slaves had in the past been sold—and whipped, as occasion demanded. There was just one moderately large house in which the slaves' overseer and his family had lived and in which the man in charge of the workers still lived today. The village was composed of a mixture of one-room hovels and some two-story buildings with outside brick staircases, looking like prison blocks. These were the dwellings in which the slaves had lived years ago and which their descendants still occupy. The houses were more dilapidated than in the days when those who dwelt in them were the legal property of the estate; otherwise, life had not changed. There were members of the same families living in the same way, working in the same sugar fields, with their fate, as before, completely in the hands of those who owned the land—but lacking now the relative security of slaves.

Pedro's home was one of a group of windowless one-room huts. The only light came through the open door. It had an uneven dirt floor trodden hard by bare feet over the centuries. In the corner was a crumbling brick structure on which generations of slave women had done their cooking and where Pedro still cooked his food today; there was neither water, lighting, kitchen, nor lavatory.

One could make an inventory of all Pedro's worldly goods at a single glance. There was just a hammock tied to the wall and a little stool made from the stump of a tree. But Pedro had two unusual possessions. One was his old umbrella. He was, he explained, a bachelor, and so it had been possible for him to save up for it. It gave him protection from the rain in the wet season and from the sun for the rest of the year. And, exceptionally, too, there was a cardboard box full of books. Across it were printed in large letters those well-intentioned words which so often humiliate and cause offense to the poor of three continents: "Donated by the people of the U.S.A." It had once held American relief goods.

"Food for death" is what the sugar workers call it. In their direct, simple way they say that the sugar which they slave to produce goes to the people of the United States who determine its price. This is so low that it keeps the sugar workers in their present poverty. The food is, therefore, a conscience gift, a substitute for justice.

Pedro had filled his box with his little library. This consisted of the few paper-covered textbooks he required as a radio school monitor, and three hard-cover books. Two of these were by now well-thumbed; one, his latest acquisition, was new. All three had been published by the Jehovah Witnesses.

He was a Catholic, and he knew that their religion was not his. But these people had been good enough to give him the books. Although he had never been to school, he had learned to read and write from a friend years ago and somehow he wanted to be able to satisfy the hunger of his mind. These books provided him with his one opportunity.

On the wall, close against the low ceiling which had been blackened by centuries of oil and candle smoke, hung a blackboard. His home might be indistinguishable from the hovels which surround it, just as, apart from his umbrella, he was almost indistinguishable from his fellow workers in the sugar fields. But by night when the people of the village came to gather round MEB's little transistor radio, his hut became a school: he became their teacher, and they were his pupils. True, the real teacher was the voice which came over the radio from Recife. But Pedro made the voice human, made comprehensible to them what the teacher had to say, as he wrote on his blackboard and encouraged them to do the same.

By virtue of this relationship with his neighbors and fellow workers, and by virtue, too, of the fact that for long he had been the first and only man among them who could read, he was their leader. MEB had now developed the latent qualities of leadership which equipped him for that position.

Near to the row of huts was a little plot on which the people were able to grow a few vegetables. This, they explained to me, was tolerated, but not approved. Even so, they felt privileged. Quite frequently sugar workers who must live in tiny corners of plantations of tens of thousands of acres are denied a single square yard on which to grow a bean plant or two. The plantation owner often operates the infamous truck system; he owns the only shop, and at this they are obliged to make all their purchases. This, in effect, means that they are forever in debt to him and so his hold over them is absolute.

The workers in Pedro's village were, like the woman to whom I had talked earlier, putting in only three or four days' work a week. The factory and refinery, as I had seen, had come to a standstill. The workers had no idea what was happening. Pedro believed that the owners were either about to go bankrupt or were just marking time to see which way the government's economic policies were going to go. But the sugar crop was valuable; it was necessary that it should be weeded, because otherwise it would be lost. And so he and his neighbors were working for three or four days a week. None of them had been paid for many weeks now. No representative of the owners had been seen for some time, but the workers had decided that, unless they saved the crop, all would be lost and they might find themselves homeless as well as wageless.

They had gone to their agriculture workers' union for help, but had been told that there was nothing the union could do. They had returned with just one box of dried milk. The milk had long since been used. The box was the one that now housed Pedro's three books.

ARCHBISHOP OF THE WOODEN CROSS

"This is not a human situation. If you travel through our rural areas, you will see that the condition of the people is terrible. Like men everywhere, they long to live in peace. But the only way to arrive at peace is through justice, and these people are the victims of injustice."

The speaker was Archbishop Helder Câmara, perhaps the best known of Brazil's "wooden cross" bishops. Dom Helder is slight, frail-looking, restless. When he came to see me, he was, as usual, dressed in an old black clerical suit; around his neck was a cheap metal chain from which hung a small, plain wooden cross.

On the eve of the second session of the Vatican Council, when he was Archbishop of Rio de Janeiro, Dom Helder wrote a paper entitled "An Exchange of Ideas with Our Brothers in the Episcopate" which was circulated among the bishops of the world. In it he stressed that a return to poverty is "more important than the examination of points of doctrine." He listed a number of proposals for discussion. Among these was one that such titles as "Excellency" and "Eminence" should be suppressed; so, too, should be the use of coats of arms and mottoes. These things, he wrote, separate us "especially from the workers and the poor."

The archbishop urged caution in the wearing of expensive pectoral crosses and rings. Silver-buckle shoes he described as "ridiculous and out of place today." And he went on to urge his brother bishops not to "make our moral strength and our authority depend on the make of our car." For the closing Mass of the Council, Dom Helder made a suggestion which was not taken up. This was that the bishops should place at the feet of Pope Paul their gold and silver pectoral crosses. In exchange each would receive one of bronze or wood.

During the 28 years he was in Rio, he came to be loved by many, particularly the poor, and hated by a few, particularly the rich. In Rio, I had been variously told that he was a Communist, a fellow-traveler, a willing tool of the Reds, an agitator, an incredibly irresponsible ecclesiastic. And a saint!

"So long as I remain busy in my sacristy," he told me, "people say, 'Dom Helder, he's a saint'. But when I come out of my sacristy to work for human progress, they say, 'Dom Helder is a Communist'. For example, when I try to prepare the poor people who are in my care for the material, social, intellectual, and spiritual development which is needed. Our movement for basic education is good, but its most important task is to open the eyes of the people to their true situation. To make them see the need for human conditions in which to live. To see that it is only through organization, through trade unions, and rural syndicates, that they will have any opportunity of talking to the rich as men talking to men.

"If the government is willing to help to create a situation where this is possible, then there will be peace in Brazil. But if the military government stops the activity which has grown out of our attempts to open the eyes of the people, then it is going to be faced with great difficulties, and it will make great difficulties for us. The United States will create problems for itself, as well as for us, too, if it continues to pursue, and to recommend to our government, policies which are just as selfish as those of Russia, and are aimed only at keeping Latin America safe for the United States and its trading policies."

Dom Helder explained to me why he believed that he as an archbishop, and the Church, too, should be stripped of all privilege.

"When I read the Gospels as a child, I thought that there was a certain exaggeration in Christ's words about the spiritual condition of the rich, when, for example, he said that it was easier for a camel to go through the eye of a needle than for a rich man to get into heaven. Now I have come to see that the absence of vision by the rich is a most terrible thing. I am amazed that the lessons taught by history have not been learned by rich men here in Brazil and elsewhere."

I asked him whether he was afraid that the organizations started by MEB and encouraged by the Church might be infiltrated by Communists. There were people in Rio who said that this was the situation before the military coup occurred. What had he to say to this?

He replied: "We must fight Communism with economic and social development, fight it by fighting injustice, particularly among the poor. The Communists have no great following among the rural people. If, here and there, they have seized the leadership, it is because we ourselves have not produced the necessary leaders. Perhaps they have had some success with a few of the students. But we must appeal to those students to whom Communism appeals. We must fight Communism with truth, with intelligence, and by appealing directly to their souls. Yes, of course, we have Communists at work in Brazil, but most of them are not really Communists. They are fighting injustice and inhuman conditions." To make sure that I got his point, he took my notes and wrote into them: "Communists in Brazil? Yes. But two-thirds of them are men desiring justice. We must discover through our mistakes the soul of truth."

"But how about the remaining one-third?" I asked. "They are the hard-core Communists and the leaders. They know what they are doing, where they are going. They are dialectical materialists operating from an entirely different set of basic principles and values than those of the Christian. On the basis of my own knowledge of Communists in every part of the world I can accept that they are in good faith. But I also know that they believe that they have neither to accept nor to adhere to the Christian rules. They can use whatever means they please so long as these serve the cause of Communism. What do we do about them?"

"The responsibility is ours, not theirs," the gentle, unassuming prelate replied. "Today they cannot see the truth of the faith because of the wealth of Christians and the riches and organization of the Church. We need to realize the moral power of the Vatican. This has been smothered and suffocated by the history of the Papal States, the Church's temporal power, her material riches, by the organization of Vatican diplomats, and all the trappings of a State dealing with other States. It is the Church's wealth in particular that is the stumbling block. We must make the Church we love such that all men can see that this is the Church of the poor. When this happens, there will be no Communism, no Communists."

Dom Helder, small, frail, ascetic, dynamic, works and lives on impulse. He would be the despair, as was Pope John XXIII, of anyone who tried to organize his time and activities. Unlike the government, he does not have to find an answer to the problem of runaway inflation. He does not have to rule a country. He sees his huge homeland, with its untapped and almost unlimited resources, struggling for survival in a fast-developing but tumultuous world. He has seen, as a result of his travels, the appalling contrast between the wealth of the rich neighbor to the north and the poverty of Brazil. He has seen the equally startling contrast between the extremes of wealth to be found in Brazil's great cities and the almost unbelievable poverty and degradation of the people of the slums of those same cities and, on a mass scale, of the people of the Northeast where he now has his greatest responsibility.

For him it is self-evident that the Church's most urgent message today is for the poor, for justice for the poor. Until they have been lifted out of their degrading conditions and given a ticket to life, the Church's message must fall on deaf ears, her representatives look like so many hypocrites. Dom Helder Câmara and the other wooden-cross bishops are necessary to the conscience of Brazil, necessary to the conscience of all who call themselves Christians. To the politicians, the economists, particularly to the professional and pathological anti-Communists, he is at best wildly impractical, at worst a menace.

You cannot, of course, argue with him. You do not argue with a saint, least of all with one who is so clearly prepared to sacrifice himself utterly and completely for those who are most in need.

I saw Dom Helder out of my hotel, then bought a newspaper. There, on the front page, was a photograph of a long wall bordering the archbishop's residence on which had been scrawled overnight a slogan which read "Viva B.C.P. Viva Dom Helder." B.C.P. is of course the Communist party of Brazil.

The slogan may have been painted by Communist cadres cynically intent upon linking his name with theirs. It might have been painted by one of those Communists who are the "two-thirds" to whom he had referred, who desire justice and see no conflict between support for what little they know of Communism and for Dom Helder whose goodness has caught their imagination.

Or, of course, it might possibly have been the work of provocateurs of the lunatic fringe of the Right, out to smear and to hurt under cover of darkness.

Either way, it underlined the difficulty of the man who, intent upon following Christ in deed as well as in word, sets out to end injustice in the mid-twentieth century. One thing is certain, and that is that Dom Helder Câmara will continue to be the subject of attack from both Left and Right. But I doubt if that thought causes Dom Helder to lose any sleep. It is much more likely that the thought of the 30 million people who live in poverty in Brazil's Northeast keeps him awake at nights.

THE COMMUNISTS' PROBLEMS

Now that he is an old man, Luis Carlos Prestes, leader of Brazil's Communist party, must look back somewhat wistfully over the years. A man of considerable charm and impressive personal integrity, as a young army officer, in the 1920's, he turned his back on the officer class into which he was born and accepted the hazardous life of a guerilla leader. His long trek through the jungle, leading a column of dissident army officers and others for years on end, is something of a saga in itself. In due course, he joined the Communist party of which he was before long made Secretary-General.

Being a Communist leader in a country living under a dictatorship was a dangerous business. Prestes had years of exile in Russia, more years in the underground with a price on his head. For nine years he was in prison. Then, in the wave of democratic fervor which swept Brazil and so many other countries of Latin America at the end of World War II, he emrged from jail to become a senator and to see his small party grow to one of 150,000 members which could attract more than half a million votes in democratic elections.

Right at the beginning of the cold war, when the Russian leaders believed that the Soviet Union was threatened with military attack, Stalin called upon Communist leaders everywhere to come out and declare that they would urge the working class to support the Soviet Union against their own governments in the event of war. This was a turning point in the fortunes of a number of European Communist parties. Luis Carlos Prestes did as he was requested, and this total identification with the U.S.S.R. on the part of what the public had supposed to be a strongly nationalistic party, proved to be a turning point for the B.C.P. too.

As has been seen, Goulart's muddle-headed, inefficient, "progressive" regime created a situation which, had the party been strong enough to exploit it, might well have led on to Communism. Instead, when the moment of opportunity came, the membership of the party was fewer than 40,000. These included a good proportion of dedicated, well-trained cadres, but they did not add up to a force capable of leading a revolution in a country the size of Brazil.

Moreover, the Communist movement was by now divided. The official Communist party was strongly pro-Moscow; this meant that it was laying its main emphasis upon the "peaceful road to socialism." Against this a minority rebelled and in due course formed their own pro-Castro and pro-Peking parties. Today these rival Communist parties, along with Trotskyist and national-Marxist groups, compete for the allegiance of militant students, workers, and peasants.

Brazil's Communists have for years devoted themselves to infiltrating trade unions, peasant unions, and also the other political parties. They have succeeded in creating or attaching themselves to one popular front after another. In most countries, use of the united front tactic tends to lead to the growth of the Communist party as the expense of the others, but in Brazil the opposite has frequently been the case. The parties and student organizations which have associated with it have thrived and grown on the basis of work done by tireless, dedicated Communist cadres. This has even included the Catholic student organization, *Juventude Universitária Católica*.

The Communists have suffered, too, from the fact that

practically every party in the land, apart from semi-Fascist ones, is left of center, and most talk the language of revolution. Whether deliberately or not, they thus steal the Communists' thunder. Moreover, the Communists suffer under the disability of known allegiance to some outside power, whether it be Moscow, Peking, or Cuba.

Because the Communists have infiltrated, at one time or another, practically every progressive organization in the land, including Church-inspired ones, they have brought under suspicion organizations which work for legitimate change and have discredited genuinely democratic movements. They have thus made it more difficult for political Christian Democracy of the new type to get established. The situation is not helped by episodes such as that which occurred in August, 1966, when several battalions of infantry sent by the government broke up a clandestine conference of the radical Catholic *União Nacional de Estudantes* meeting in Franciscan and Dominican friaries.

Even so, democratic Christian organizations like MEB are successfully operating in fields which in the past were left to the Communists. If these are permitted to continue their activities unimpeded by the government, a genuinely non-Marxist progressive movement may in time emerge.

The Four-Hundred-Year Lag

9

Latin America's struggle to catch up with what has been called "the four-hundred-year lag" is one of the great dramas of our time. The fate of a sub-continent and 200,-000,000 people hangs upon its outcome. To suggest that the choice is simply between Catholicism and Communism is to oversimplify to the point of distortion. It looked like this some years ago. Today it is apparent that there are other alternatives.

Latin America could continue to be a continental slum, but a capitalist one instead of a feudal one. It would, indeed, be tragic if, after struggling for years to break their feudal shackles, the people should find themselves living in nothing better than a materialistic, third-rate, industrial society. Yet this could happen.

There is already a good deal of evidence to show that Latin America will most probably develop along its own lines. Even though the process of change is still only in its beginnings, it is already fairly clear that whatever social system replaces the present one, it is unlikely to follow exactly a pattern of life evolved elsewhere. Latin Americans do not readily adopt the jukebox culture which U.S. tourists and, particularly, the American armed forces, have tended to take with them wherever they have gone. And they are not likely to adopt a U.S.-type free enterprise society either, no matter how much American aid is poured into their countries—and no matter how successfully free enterprise may flourish in the soil of the United States. North Americans may comfort themselves with the thought that this same tendency on the part of their Latin neighbors makes them equally resistant to social systems which have their origins in Russia or China.

What in material terms Latin America requires most urgently and above all else is change in the socio-economic structure, in short, social revolution. Peaceful revolution, even less than violent revolution, cannot be imported. It must come from within, even though some practical aid and encouragement can be given to the process from outside.

This is not a job for the Alliance for Progress. It is a task for Latin Americans themselves. The future of the Alliance was in any case from the start in the hands of the very classes who would suffer most from social change. To strengthen the position of those who represent the greatest possible barrier to change is no way to bring it about, just as backing any sort of tyrant, dictator, or demagogue so long as he calls himself anti-Communist is no way to fight Communism. Again, social progress is impeded, not helped, when anyone who demands change is at once branded a Communist. It may require some degree of political sophistication to understand that it is possible that even some of those who take to the gun and form guerilla bands in Latin

America may not necessarily be Communists either—although some undoubtedly are.

When new groups of guerillas in Bolivia came into the news early in 1967, Bolivian sources immediately described them as Communists. But Bolivia has had many guerilla fighters in recent years who, even though they might be described either as radical or as left, were not Communists. Some hesitation should be shown before anyone confidently attaches the Communist label to the latest group driven to desperation by impossibly frustrating situations.

Without fundamental social change, aid can at best be effective only to a limited extent. It can bring first aid to those in desperate need. But it cannot be put to best use so long as the structure of Latin American society remains as it is.

If aid is to be given, it should be because there are people, fellow human beings, in need, not as part of some scheme to improve the image of the donor country, save the people of the area from going "Red," or impose some alien way of life upon them. Recent history tends to show that any attempt to direct the course of change from outside is likely to prove disastrous and to have the opposite effect. But given the necessary aid, Latin American countries may evolve a new society which is distinctively their own and which may well prove to have much to contribute to the evolution of other countries.

Because of the existence of widespread illiteracy and poverty, there are many problems which, at this stage of its development, Latin America is incapable of solving single-handed. But given specialists, technicians, and know-how, Latin America should before very long be able to move forward under its own steam.

The amount of aid which has come in recent years from the United States is already substantial, though it is trivial when considered in the light of North American potentialities and Latin American needs. Perhaps more significant than any material aid which has been given has been the generous spirit which has motivated many of the volunteers who have gone south to lend a hand. They have impressed people wherever they have gone with their sincerity and idealism. But I hope that I am not being unduly harsh when I say that, useful though their efforts have been, these have so far helped a) the volunteers themselves, b) the groups from which they have come—by raising the idealistic sights of the whole group, c) the image of the United States, d) the people at the receiving end. In that order! This is not to minimize the value of the aid which they have given. But I do suggest that if it is to move out of the "enthusiastic amateur" phase, the order will have to be changed.

A startling feature about the aid efforts so far, whether considered singly or collectively, is their hit-or-miss, haphazard character. The goods and the people tend to go, not necessarily where the need is greatest, but where someone makes the most noise or has the best sense of public relations. I have cooperated with at least half a dozen different American aid schemes and projects which have sent splendid, idealistic, immensely keen volunteers to Latin America. But as one travels around, one is left asking whether they are making the maximum impact. Are they doing all they might do? Are they going to the places where they can be of greatest use? Have they the right skills?

I would not pretend to be in a position to be able to weigh the needs of one area as opposed to another, still less to judge the value of various human groups and the urgency of their needs. But narrowing it down to the Catholic effort, one is left feeling that perhaps a point is being reached where an overall scheme for the whole area is needed, so that people with the right skills should be got to the places where they are most urgently required. As things stand at the moment, it is often all too apparent that those who have the greatest enthusiasm frequently lack what Latin America needs most. No one is helped when, for example, a group of eager young teachers from abroad voluntarily staffs a primary school in an area where there are already local teachers desperately looking for work. This sort of thing happens too often.

From my most recent travels in Latin America, I returned with a strong impression that the Germans, who are taking an increasing interest in the area, are probably getting the biggest and best returns for the money and personnel they put into their projects. On the basis of careful preliminary inquiries, they discover the area of greatest need, then seek out the right people regardless of nationality (and frequently these may be locals) and support them right up to the hilt. It was U.S. Vice-President Hubert Humphrey who spoke of "the remarkable success" of "indigenous specialized institutions" in Chile which "can be credited to the unified, systematic program of regular financial support provided by the German Bishops' Fund which now raises eight million dollars per year for Latin America." It is perhaps time that someone in the United States did an in-depth study of Latin American needs, and concentrated upon locating and channeling the people who are best qualified to meet those needs.

Something similar is required by the Church as the

number of priests from North America and Europe steadily builds up. Again, we find the same hit-or-miss approach and the same need for an overall plan. The Church is fortunate in that it already has an organization, CELAM, which thinks and organizes on a continental scale.

If Christians and others have their problems, it is consoling to know that Latin America's Communists clearly have theirs. Things do not necessarily go as the Communists would wish. Cuba raised the hopes of Moscow, and Peking, and of the Communist parties throughout Latin America. For Russia to underwrite the Cuban economy made sense if Castro's revolution was going to touch off other revolutions in more significant countries on the mainland, such as, for example, Venezuela. But it has probably long since ceased to make sense in Soviet eyes because no such revolutions have followed. Instead, Castro has lost his romantic appeal; the pro-Communist flames which suddenly leapt into the air from one end of Latin America to the other are now little more than flickers. Even so, there is far too much combustible material lying around for anyone's peace of mind.

A single issue of the *Peking Review* could report the following:

"In Guatemala the insurgent army vigorously consolidated its bases in the mountain areas and mobilized the peasants . . .

"In Colombia, peasant guerilla engagements broke out afresh in the Marquetalia region . . . 'mopping-up' operations were smashed in which 16,000 troops took part under American command . . .

"In Nicaragua, under the rule of a pro-U.S. dictatorial

regime, the revolutionary armed struggle led by the Sandino National Liberation Front is still going on.

"In Venezuela, the National Liberation Army successfully frustrated several U.S.-directed 'mopping-up' operations and developed its guerilla war in the countryside . . .

". . . peasants in the mountainous region of the Piura Province in Northern Peru succeeded in seizing fifteen plantations . . . To protest against the massacre of peasants fighting for land by the government army and police force, 15,000 Peruvian peasants of Sicuani, a city in Cusco Province, marched into the provincial capital . . ."

The *Peking Review* was, however, reviewing the year 1964 and was making the most of what Latin American Communists had to offer. Only a year or two earlier, both Peking and Moscow were hoping for more than this. They must be expected to keep on trying. The coming years may well prove that more important to the Communist cause than the first flush of enthusiasm for Castro is the current training of hundreds of volunteers in guerilla warfare and urban terrorism by Cuba and China.

The extent to which the Communists succeed or fail, will undoubtedly be determined to a considerable extent by the success or failure of the new Christian Democracy and by the sort of leadership which comes from the Church at every level.

A few years ago, before Vatican Council II, a Vatican diplomat told me that something as profound as the Reformation in Europe was happening to the Church in Latin America. Catholic losses to Protestantism, he said, were on such a scale that the entire sub-continent could be lost to the faith within a generation. Something more important than a Catholic-Protestant squabble is at stake today. The need for a truly Christian approach to social problems by Christians of any hue is urgent and imperative.

Catholics have no cause for complaint if Protestants move into areas which for generations on end have, for whatever reason, been left priestless, or if they bring Christianity to people whom the Church has already lost because of its too close identification with the privileged classes. This should not be seen as some sort of outrage against the Church, but as a direct challenge to Catholics inside Latin America and elsewhere, a challenge to recognize the need for Christian unity and, above all else, to give a Christian lead on social questions which, in the very nature of the case, must take priority in people's minds. It is also a challenge to engage in ecumenical effort in an area of the world where misunderstandings and openly un-Christian rivalry between competing Christian bodies have been all too common.

A real danger to Christianity is that Latin America might free itself from the last remnants of primitive paganism only to become ensnared in some form of that modern paganism which so often emerges when a country achieves material prosperity at the price of spiritual poverty.

The problem of which the largest number of people in Latin America are most keenly aware today is that of their own material poverty. There can be little doubt that the Church will reach the proletarianized masses of the urban slums and the impoverished people of the rural areas most easily if it can break away from its traditional identification with the oligarchy and come to be seen as, in Pope John's words, "the Church of the poor."

"How difficult it is for us poor bishops of Christ's Church," said Bishop Juan J. Iriarte of Reconquista, Argentina, "to put across in the twentieth century this message which in origin is stamped by the poverty of the Incarnation, of the crib and the cross. That message today is meant to reach men of mass austerity and proletarian poverty—65 per cent of whom are hungry and a part of whom live in the slums, in 'favelas,' in 'shanty towns' of big and strange cities.

"These people call each other 'comrade' and are used to the sharp, direct language of their leaders . . . we have to deliver our message from the marble heights of our altars and episcopal palaces. . . . And, then, we go to meet our people in the latest model car all dressed in purple; the people come to us saying 'Your Excellency' as they kneel to kiss the stone of our rings. To free oneself from all the weight of history and custom is not easy. . . . But, Lord, grant us the humility, poverty, and simplicity of heart to guide the Church in our twentieth century that it may realize the simple ideal proposed to it by your humble son, John, 'that it be the Church of the poor.' "

Or, as the bishops of Chile put it when they were discussing, in one of their many social doctrine statements, the need for the transformation of the social structure and the spiritual renewal of the people: what is needed above all else is "a change of mentality and spirituality."

Epilogue

Outside his hut on the sugar plantation in Pernambuco, with the slave church, the slave block, and the slave dwellings around him, Pedro, descendant of slaves, was wishing me goodbye.

A few months earlier I had smashed a thumb in a car door. Now the blackened nail was being pushed up and out by a new one.

Pedro took my hand in his. "See," he said, "the new is pushing out what is old and dead. Soon there will be something good and healthy to take the place of what is bad. That is like my country. What is old and dead is beginning to be pushed out by what is good and new.

"The change must come. It is already beginning."

Index

217